INVENTIONS

Written by
ERYL DAVIES

OCTANT
(c.1750)

GRAMOPHONE
(EARLY 1900S)

TECHNICOLOR
CAMERA (1932)

DORLING KINDERSLEY
London • New York • Stuttgart

A DORLING KINDERSLEY BOOK

Project editor Mary-Clare Mitchell
Art editor Louise Morley
Senior editor Laura Buller
Senior art editor Helen Senior
Editorial consultant Susan Watt
Picture research Giselle Harvey
Production Louise Barratt
Catherine Semark

First published in Great Britain in 1995
by Dorling Kindersley Limited
9 Henrietta Street, Covent Garden, London WC2E 8PS

Reprinted 1996

Copyright © 1995 Dorling Kindersley Ltd., London

A CIP catalogue record for this book is available from
the British Library.

ISBN 0 7513 5184 9

Colour reproduction by Colourscan, Singapore
Printed and bound in Italy by L.E.G.O.

CONTENTS

HOW TO USE THIS BOOK

These pages show you how to use *Pockets: Inventions*. The book is divided into several sections. The main section gives detailed information about hundreds of inventions. There is also an introductory section at the front, and a reference section at the back. Turn to the contents or index pages for more information.

INVENTIONS

The inventions in the book have been grouped into related subjects and arranged into five sections – Everyday Life, Trade and Industry, Science and Communication, Travel and Exploration, and Entertainment and Leisure. An introduction page at the beginning of each section gives an overview of the pages that follow.

Corner coding

Heading

Introduction

Caption

SCIENCE AND COMMUNICATION

OPTICAL INVENTIONS

MICROSCOPES, TELESCOPES, and other optical inventions have been vital for advances in science. Most optical devices contain lenses, which can make small objects appear larger or distant objects appear closer. Lenses depend on the fact that rays of light bend, or refract, as they pass from air to glass.

Observer looks here

Sliding focus

WATCHING THE STARS
The first telescope was built in 1608 by Dutchman Hans Lippershey. It had two lenses that refracted the light and made distant objects look much closer. A year later, Italian Galileo Galilei used a similar telescope to study the Moon.

Telescope rests on wooden ball

NEWTON'S REFLECTOR (1668)

MAGNIFYING WITH MIRRORS
In 1668, Isaac Newton built the first reflecting telescope, which used curved mirrors instead of lenses to magnify distant objects. Newton's reflective produced much clearer images than refracting telescopes of the time.

GALILEO'S TELESCOPE (EARLY 17TH CENTURY)

Label

HEADING

This describes the subject of the page. This page is about optical inventions. If a subject continues over several pages, the same heading applies.

INTRODUCTION

This provides a clear, general overview of the subject. After reading the introduction, you should have an idea of what the pages are about.

LABELS

For extra clarity, some pictures have labels. These give extra information, or identify a picture when it is not obvious from the text what it is.

FACT BOXES

Many pages in the introductory and main sections have fact boxes. These contain at-a-glance information and provide extra facts about the subject. This fact box gives more details about optical inventions and discoveries.

RUNNING HEADS

These remind you which section you are in. The top of the left-hand page gives the section name. The right-hand page gives the subject. This page on optical inventions is in the Science and Communication section.

Running head

Annotation

Fact box

REFERENCE SECTION

The reference section pages are yellow and appear at the back of the book. On these pages, you will find useful facts, dates, and charts, including an A-Z of inventors, a timeline of inventions, and maps of great inventing civilizations.

CAPTIONS AND ANNOTATIONS

Each illustration has a caption and most have annotations. Annotations, in *italics*, point out features of an illustration and usually have leader lines.

INDEX

There are two indexes at the back of the book – a subject index, and an index of inventors. The subject index lists each subject covered in the book. The index of inventors lists the inventors that are featured.

INTRODUCTION
TO INVENTIONS

WHAT IS AN INVENTION?

AN INVENTION IS THE CREATION of something that didn't exist before. It can be a simple gadget, a novel process, a new material, or a complex machine. Some inventions result from the desire to fulfil specific needs; others arise by accident or evolve gradually. The bicycle, for example, is not a single invention but a combination of many individual inventions.

MODERN HYBRID
BICYCLE

Saddle

*Adjustable
seat post*

Welded joints

*Brakes were
first used in
the 1860s.*

THE BICYCLE
Many inventions, from one of the earliest (the wheel) to one of the most recent (the composite frame) can be found in a modern bicycle.

*Taut wire spokes
were added to
bicycle wheels
in 1870.*

Gears

WHEELS
Originally made of either wood or stone, wheels were invented by the Mesopotamians more than 5,000 years ago.

*Chains were first
used in 1869.*

*Gear mechanism was
patented in 1896*

CHAINS AND GEARS
The addition of chains and gears made bicycles much easier to ride. The chain allows the pedals to be positioned under the seat rather than on the front wheel, while gears enable the cyclist to ride at different speeds while pedalling normally.

Changing gear moves the chain from one cog to another.

Handlebar

Brake cables were devised by Ernest Bowden in 1896.

annondale

Strong, lightweight frame

NEW MATERIALS
The earliest bicycle frames were made from wood and iron and were very cumbersome. Lighter steel frames were introduced in the 1890s, while tough composite materials appeared much more recently.

Quick-release lever

Tread enables tyre to grip the road

Pneumatic (air-filled) tyres were invented in 1888.

Pedals appeared in 1839 and originally had to be pushed to and fro.

Valve for filling tyre with air

WHY DO PEOPLE INVENT?

PEOPLE INVENT FOR ALL KINDS of reasons. Some invent in order to meet basic human needs, while others invent to fulfil their own creative desires. Many inventions are inspired by social or economic reasons; in other words, by the desire to make life easier and more comfortable – or by the need to make money.

Meeting economic demands

Making money can be a powerful incentive for invention, allowing individuals, companies, or nations to stay ahead of the competition. During the early years of textile manufacture, for example, a succession of inventions kept the wheels of industry turning.

FLYING SHUTTLE

Shuttle holding thread

Device for throwing shuttle from right to left across loom

FLYING SHUTTLE
Weaving became much faster after Englishman John Kay invented the flying shuttle in 1733. The shuttle was thrown across the loom at high speed, taking the thread with it.

HANDLOOM WITH FLYING SHUTTLE

Drive wheel

SPINNING FRAME
The invention of the flying shuttle meant that yarn was used up much more quickly than it could be spun. To solve this problem, various inventors devised power-driven spinning machines. One such machine was this spinning frame, built by Richard Arkwright in 1769.

ARKWRIGHT'S SPINNING FRAME (1769)

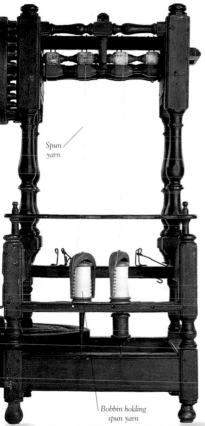

Spun yarn

Bobbin holding spun yarn

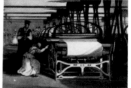

STEAM POWER
Powered spinning then led to a surplus of yarn that could not be woven quickly enough. The balance was restored in 1787, when Edmund Cartwright built the first steam-powered loom.

COTTON GIN (1792)

Raw cotton from which seeds are removed

COTTON GIN
Meanwhile, in the U.S.A., the demand for raw cotton was growing. In 1792, Eli Whitney invented the cotton gin, which separated cotton from its seeds at high speed. As a result, cotton production increased dramatically.

Meeting social needs

For thousands of years, inventions have been inspired by the basic human needs of comfort, security, hygiene, and health. More recently, devices that make life easier or more luxurious have become increasingly popular. Whatever the reason for their creation, many inventions have had a huge impact on the way we live, and our lives would be very different without them.

LOCK AND KEY
(1700S)

Lock mechanism

Iron key

End of key operates lock mechanism

Locks contain a series of levers, which are moved by the key.

Dowsing bulb gives off heat

EARLY ELECTRIC FIRE

SAFETY AND SECURITY
Many devices are invented for our safety and security. In 1818, Jeremiah Chubb designed a lock mechanism to prevent burglaries at a local naval dockyard. Sadly, modern society requires many of us to install similar devices in our own homes.

Reflector

COMFORTABLE LIVING
Inventions such as fires, heaters, and air conditioning systems have been designed to make life more comfortable, either by keeping us warm in cold weather, or by keeping us cool in hot weather.

ASPIRIN
TINS (c.1930)

STAYING HEALTHY

By eradicating infections, or providing cures for diseases, many inventions have enabled people to live longer and healthier lives. The development of drugs and vaccines, and improvements in general hygiene, have been vital in the fight against illness.

Handle

Soap powder first went on sale in 1907.

SAVING TIME AND EFFORT

The desire to save time and effort around the home has inspired the invention of the vacuum cleaner, the washing machine, and many other devices. This vacuum cleaner was built by the Hoover company in 1908.

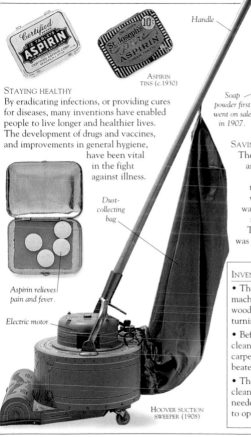

Dust-collecting bag

Aspirin relieves pain and fever.

Electric motor

HOOVER SUCTION
SWEEPER (1908)

INVENTION FACTS

• The first washing machines were simply wooden boxes with turning handles.

• Before the vacuum cleaner was invented, carpets had to be beaten to remove dust.

• The first vacuum cleaners were huge and needed several people to operate them.

THE STORY OF AN INVENTION

AN INVENTION CAN take years to develop
and can involve the combined efforts
of many different people. The story of
the sewing machine illustrates how a
simple idea can gradually evolve into
a complex machine, as new ideas and
inventions are incorporated.

MACHINE-SEWING

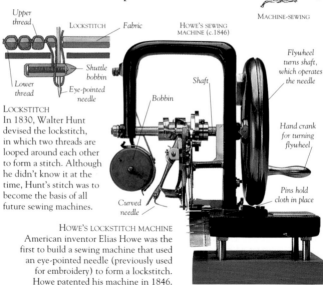

Upper thread — LOCKSTITCH — Fabric

HOWE'S SEWING MACHINE (c.1846)

Shuttle bobbin

Lower thread — Eye-pointed needle

Flywheel turns shaft, which operates the needle

Shaft

Bobbin

Hand crank for turning flywheel

Pins hold cloth in place

Curved needle

LOCKSTITCH

In 1830, Walter Hunt
devised the lockstitch,
in which two threads are
looped around each other
to form a stitch. Although
he didn't know it at the
time, Hunt's stitch was to
become the basis of all
future sewing machines.

HOWE'S LOCKSTITCH MACHINE

American inventor Elias Howe was the
first to build a sewing machine that used
an eye-pointed needle (previously used
for embroidery) to form a lockstitch.
Howe patented his machine in 1846.

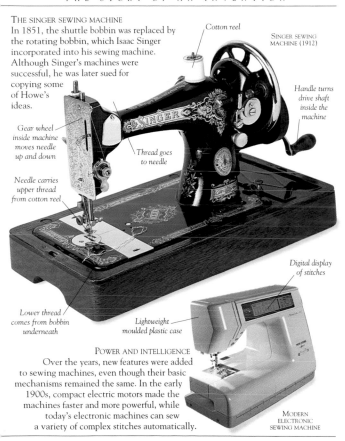

THE SINGER SEWING MACHINE

In 1851, the shuttle bobbin was replaced by the rotating bobbin, which Isaac Singer incorporated into his sewing machine. Although Singer's machines were successful, he was later sued for copying some of Howe's ideas.

Cotton reel

SINGER SEWING MACHINE (1912)

Handle turns drive shaft inside the machine

Gear wheel inside machine moves needle up and down

Thread goes to needle

Needle carries upper thread from cotton reel

Lower thread comes from bobbin underneath

Lightweight moulded plastic case

Digital display of stitches

POWER AND INTELLIGENCE

Over the years, new features were added to sewing machines, even though their basic mechanisms remained the same. In the early 1900s, compact electric motors made the machines faster and more powerful, while today's electronic machines can sew a variety of complex stitches automatically.

MODERN ELECTRONIC SEWING MACHINE

FAILED INVENTIONS

INVENTIONS ARE OFTEN UNSUCCESSFUL. Some simply don't work because of a basic flaw in the inventor's understanding or knowledge. Others fail to catch on because, despite their ingenuity, they don't actually save any time or effort. Many are unreliable, expensive, or totally impractical.

EDISON'S TELEPHONE

Blades spin to create breeze

Mouthpiece

Earpiece

Handle

GAS-POWERED FAN

HOT-AIR FAN
This extraordinary fan was made in 1904. Although the fan was designed to cool the air, the gas-powered motor actually gave out more heat than the fan could remove.

Edison's telephone could be mounted on the wall.

MAKING A CALL
Thomas Edison devised this telephone in 1878. Unfortunately, turning the handle made such a noise that it was almost impossible to hear what the person at the other end was saying.

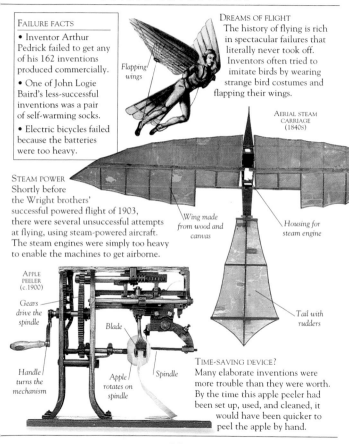

FAILURE FACTS

• Inventor Arthur Pedrick failed to get any of his 162 inventions produced commercially.

• One of John Logie Baird's less-successful inventions was a pair of self-warming socks.

• Electric bicycles failed because the batteries were too heavy.

DREAMS OF FLIGHT

The history of flying is rich in spectacular failures that literally never took off. Inventors often tried to imitate birds by wearing strange bird costumes and flapping their wings.

Flapping wings

AERIAL STEAM CARRIAGE (1840S)

STEAM POWER

Shortly before the Wright brothers' successful powered flight of 1903, there were several unsuccessful attempts at flying, using steam-powered aircraft. The steam engines were simply too heavy to enable the machines to get airborne.

Wing made from wood and canvas

Housing for steam engine

APPLE PEELER (c.1900)

Gears drive the spindle

Blade

Handle turns the mechanism

Apple rotates on spindle

Spindle

Tail with rudders

TIME-SAVING DEVICE?

Many elaborate inventions were more trouble than they were worth. By the time this apple peeler had been set up, used, and cleaned, it would have been quicker to peel the apple by hand.

EVERYDAY LIFE

INTRODUCTION

INVENTIONS PLAY A HUGE PART in our everyday lives, either by providing us with the things we need to live comfortably and healthily, or by saving us precious time and effort as we carry out our daily tasks.

HOME COMFORTS
The need for warmth has inspired many ingenious inventions. From wood-burning stoves to electric fires, people have found many different ways to heat their homes. This electric fire has a series of fine wires that heat up when electricity flows through them.

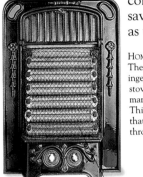

ELECTRIC FIRE
(1913)

Wires give off heat

TIMESAVERS
For many people, life has been made easier by the invention of clever gadgets that make light work of tedious chores. From tin openers to tea-makers, there are now hundreds of devices that save time around the home.

TEA-MAKER
(1904)

Bell rings when tea is ready

Clock

Tipping kettle

Spring

HEALTHY LIVING
Good sanitation and water supplies are essential for healthy living. Inventions such as the flushing toilet and sewage systems are vital for public health, especially in crowded cities.

CLOTHING
Clothes originally evolved from a need for people to protect themselves against cold or wet weather. But many modern garments, such as the brassiere, were invented to fulfil more specific needs.

FLUSHING TOILET (1800s)

Wooden seat

China bowl

Water flushes in from under the rim.

U-bend

BRASSIERES (1930s)

JAPANESE LANTERN CLOCK

Balance bar

TIMEKEEPING
Many inventions, from sundials to spring-wound watches, enable us to tell the time more accurately.

Clarence Birdseye patented fast-frozen food in 1929.

FOOD
Freezing, canning, and other preserving techniques mean that foods can now be kept for much longer and transported much farther.

BIRDS EYE
FROSTED FOODS
BRUSSELS SPROUTS
NET WEIGHT 10 OZ.
BIRDS EYE FOODS LTD.
UNILEVER HOUSE, LONDON E.C.4.

FROZEN VEGETABLES

2 5

HOMES AND BUILDINGS

HALF A MILLION years ago, people lived in huts that they made out of twigs and branches. By 10,000 B.C., some civilizations were using earth and stone to build more permanent homes. Since then, the invention of different materials, tools, and building techniques has made life much easier for builders, decorators, and do-it-yourself enthusiasts.

Wedge-shaped blocks fit closely together

Overlapping roof tiles help to keep out the rain.

MAKING AN ENTRY
The slabs of stone used above entrances to ancient buildings were heavy and difficult to lift into position. Arches, made from smaller blocks, were easier to build. The first arches appeared in Mesopotamia about 5,000 years ago.

Mortar holds bricks together

BRICKS AND MORTAR
Moulded bricks have been used for about 5,500 years, and the first roof tiles appeared in about 640 B.C. Mortar, a mixture of sand and cement, hardens after water has been added and is used to hold bricks together.

STRAIGHT AND LEVEL
In 1661, Jean de Melchisedech Thevenot invented the spirit level to check that surfaces were horizontal. Modern spirit levels also allow vertical and angled surfaces to be checked.

MODERN SPIRIT LEVEL

Air bubble trapped in tube of alcohol

WORKMATE
In 1961, Ron Hickman devised the Workmate, a light, portable workbench. Sceptical manufacturers thought that he would be lucky to sell a few dozen, but his idea sold for a fortune.

The Workmate folds up and is light to carry.

Work surface

THE WORKMATE

LETTING IN LIGHT
Crown glass, made by spinning bulbs of glass into sheets, was first used to make windows in 14th-century France.

EMULSION PAINT

FINISHING TOUCHES
Water-based emulsion paints were developed in Germany in the 1930s. Emulsion paints are safer to use than oil paints because they don't give off toxic fumes and they are less likely to catch fire.

BUILDING FACTS

• Ancient Egyptians used plumblines to check that their pillars were vertical.

• Cement was invented in ancient Rome.

• About 500,000 million bricks are made worldwide each year.

KEEPING WARM

FIRE WAS ONE of the most important discoveries that humans ever made. Until about 200 years ago, people living in cold places were almost totally dependent on fire for warmth. After about 1850, gas and electricity revolutionized heating and led to the invention of many new heating appliances and systems.

Spindle

Leather cord for rotating spindle

Heat created here by friction

STARTING A FIRE
This Inuit fire-stick was used about 4,000 years ago. The friction created by rotating the spindle produced intense heat and eventually started a fire.

HEATING FACTS

• The ancient Romans were the first to use underfloor heating.

• Patented in 1855, safety matches only ignite when struck against special surfaces.

• Londoner Sigismund Leoni made the first modern gas fire in 1881.

Tips covered with chemicals

Early matches were known as lucifers, meaning "light bearers".

Wooden splints

THE FIRST MATCHES
Lighting fires became much easier after the invention of matches. The first matches were made in 1827 by British chemist John Walker. They were tipped with special chemicals that caught fire when rubbed against a rough surface.

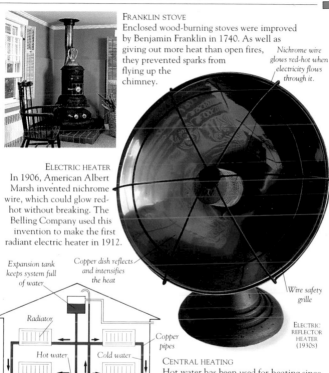

FRANKLIN STOVE
Enclosed wood-burning stoves were improved by Benjamin Franklin in 1740. As well as giving out more heat than open fires, they prevented sparks from flying up the chimney.

Nichrome wire glows red-hot when electricity flows through it.

ELECTRIC HEATER
In 1906, American Albert Marsh invented nichrome wire, which could glow red-hot without breaking. The Belling Company used this invention to make the first radiant electric heater in 1912.

Expansion tank keeps system full of water

Copper dish reflects and intensifies the heat

Radiator

Hot water   *Cold water*

Copper pipes

Gas boiler   *Electric pump circulates water*

Wire safety grille

ELECTRIC REFLECTOR HEATER
(1930s)

CENTRAL HEATING
Hot water has been used for heating since 1716, when Swede Marten Triewald used iron hot water pipes to heat greenhouses. Modern central heating systems, like this one, appeared after the development of compact electric pumps in the 1950s.

LIGHTING

ABOUT 20,000 YEARS ago, people discovered that they could produce light by burning oil. Oil lamps and candles were the main sources of artificial lighting until the early 19th century, when gas lights became more common. By the 1950s, most people were using electricity to light their homes.

Wick

SHELL LAMP

OIL BURNERS
Early people burned animal fats and vegetable oils to produce light. They used hollow shells like this to hold the fuel.

Glass cover

Oil tank

Hollow wick

Wick adjuster

OIL LAMP WITH HOLLOW WICK

Wick

CANDLELIGHT
A candle is simply a wick surrounded by tallow or wax. As the wick burns, the tallow or wax melts and gives off light. Candles appeared in Egypt about 2,000 years ago.

Wax

Snuffer extinguishes flame without giving off smoke

BURNING BRIGHT
In 1784, Frenchman Aimé Argand invented an oil lamp that had a hollow, circular wick. As air rose through the centre of the wick, the oil burned more efficiently and produced a much brighter flame.

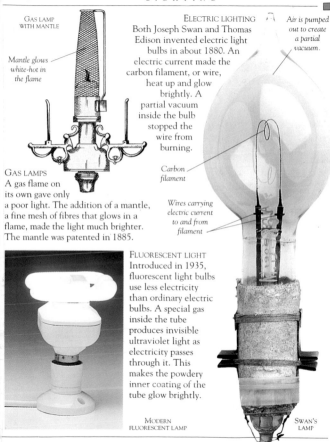

GAS LAMP
WITH MANTLE

*Mantle glows
white-hot in
the flame*

GAS LAMPS
A gas flame on
its own gave only
a poor light. The addition of a mantle,
a fine mesh of fibres that glows in a
flame, made the light much brighter.
The mantle was patented in 1885.

ELECTRIC LIGHTING
Both Joseph Swan and Thomas
Edison invented electric light
bulbs in about 1880. An
electric current made the
carbon filament, or wire,
heat up and glow
brightly. A
partial vacuum
inside the bulb
stopped the
wire from
burning.

*Air is pumped
out to create
a partial
vacuum.*

*Carbon
filament*

*Wires carrying
electric current
to and from
filament*

FLUORESCENT LIGHT
Introduced in 1935,
fluorescent light bulbs
use less electricity
than ordinary electric
bulbs. A special gas
inside the tube
produces invisible
ultraviolet light as
electricity passes
through it. This
makes the powdery
inner coating of the
tube glow brightly.

MODERN
FLUORESCENT LAMP

SWAN'S
LAMP

3 1

MAKING LIFE EASIER

IN THE PAST, many wealthy people had servants to do their domestic chores. But as more and more people started to do these chores for themselves, devices that made household tasks easier became increasingly popular.

DOING THE LAUNDRY

Around the home

Early household appliances relied on clever mechanisms to ease the job at hand. Many of these appliances were then improved with the addition of a compact electrical motor, which was invented by Nikola Tesla in 1899.

Handle

Bellows suck in dust and air

Valve

COLLECTING DUST
Most early vacuum cleaners, like this one, were operated by hand. The handle worked the bellows, which sucked dust from the carpet. The first powered vacuum cleaner was built by Hubert Cecil Booth in 1901.

Drum

Motor

FISHER'S WASHING MACHINE

WASHING MACHINE
Alva Fisher's washing machine, patented in 1907, had a drum driven by an electric motor. An automatic mechanism reversed the drum's rotation from time to time so that the clothes didn't pile up.

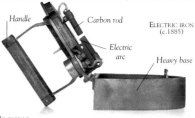

Handle — Carbon rod

ELECTRIC IRON
(c.1885)

Electric arc

Heavy base

IRONING
The electric iron was introduced by Henry Seely in 1882. It was heated by an electric arc – a powerful spark that jumped between the two carbon rods.

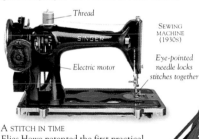

Thread

SEWING MACHINE
(1930s)

Eye-pointed needle locks stitches together

Electric motor

BUDDING'S BLADE-RUNNER
(1830)

Lever for disconnecting the gears

A STITCH IN TIME
Elias Howe patented the first practical sewing machine in 1846. The first electric sewing machine was built by Isaac Singer in 1889.

Blades

Roller

CUTTING THE GRASS
The first lawn mower was patented by Englishman Edwin Budding in 1830. The roller was connected to the blades via a series of gearwheels, which made the blades turn 12 times faster than the roller.

In the kitchen

Labour-saving devices in the kitchen are welcomed by lazy people, busy people, and keen cooks alike. Food can now be prepared and cooked more easily than ever before. As with other inventions, electricity has played a key role in the development of many kitchen appliances.

KETTLE ON
SPIRIT STOVE

Heating element

SWAN'S ELECTRIC KETTLE
Until the 1920s, electric kettles had external heating elements. But the "Swan" kettle of 1921 was more efficient because the heating element was actually in the water.

Switch to control hot plates

Electric hob

COOKING WITH ELECTRICITY
The first domestic electric cooker (stove) was made by the Carpenter Company in the U.S.A. in 1891. Gas cookers were already common, so electricity companies advertised the safety and economy of their new cookers. Even so, electric and gas cookers are now equally popular.

POP-UP TOASTER

Charles Strite, a mechanic from Minnesota, U.S.A., designed the first automatic toaster in 1927. As with modern toasters, the slices of bread rested on a spring-loaded rack and were toasted by an electric heating element. Ready-sliced bread appeared a year later.

MODERN FOOD PROCESSOR

Time control knob

Filling funnel

Motor case

PROCESSING FOOD

Compact electric motors led to the invention of numerous powered mixers and blenders. In 1971, Frenchman Pierre Verdon designed the modern food processor, with a high-speed chopping blade and electronic speed control.

Teflon's non-stick properties make light work of frying eggs.

NON-STICK FRYING

Discovered in 1941 by American Roy Plunkett, Teflon (polymerized tetrafluoroethylene) was patented for kitchenware in 1960. It is now used as a non-stick coating on all kinds of objects, from frying pans to irons.

FOOD AND DRINK

MUCH OF WHAT we eat and drink today is days, weeks, or even months old. People have devised different methods for preserving food and for ensuring that food is safe to eat. Some of these methods have been used since ancient times; others result from more recent advances in science and technology.

SALTING
A good coating of salt is one of the oldest methods for preserving fish. The salt creates an environment that discourages bacterial growth. Before it is used, the salted fish must be soaked in water.

SALTED COD

PASTEURIZATION
In 1860, Louis Pasteur found that heating wine to 70°C (158°F) killed the bacteria that caused souring. This technique is now used to treat – or pasteurize – milk.

Lid keeps tin airtight

TINNED FOOD
In 1810, Frenchman Nicolas Appert devised a way of preserving food in sealed containers. He heated the food in a glass jar and sealed the top with cork. Peter Durand developed this idea and, in 1811, produced the first tinned food.

TIN CAN

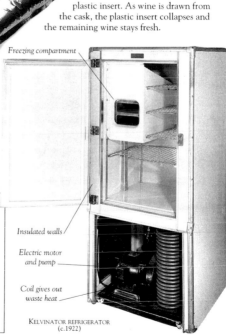

Press-button tap

WINECASK
Once a bottle of wine has been uncorked, the wine comes into contact with the air and quickly goes sour. In 1965, Australian inventor Thomas Angove solved this problem by devising the winecask, a cardboard box with a plastic insert. As wine is drawn from the cask, the plastic insert collapses and the remaining wine stays fresh.

WINECASK INSERT

Freezing compartment

KEEPING COOL
Electric refrigerators appeared in the 1920s and revolutionized food storage. A special fluid, which vaporizes at low temperatures, is pumped round pipes in the refrigerator and keeps the contents cool.

Insulated walls

Electric motor and pump

Coil gives out waste heat

KELVINATOR REFRIGERATOR
(c.1922)

FOOD FACTS

• The tin opener was not invented until 44 years after the arrival of tinned food.

• American Clarence Birdseye patented fast-frozen food in 1929.

• Engineer Ermal Fraze invented the ring-pull can in 1959.

CLOTHING

CLOTHES WERE ORIGINALLY invented to protect people against the elements. As civilizations developed, people made clothes for more specific purposes and devised ways to improve their clothes, by making them warmer, more waterproof, or simply easier to get on and off.

Plaited wool fastening

AZTEC SANDAL

Sole made from fibre of aloe plant

FOOTWEAR
Early people devised various kinds of footwear to protect their feet from hard and stony ground. Many shoes, like this Aztec sandal, were made from plant fibres.

ZIPPING UP
In 1893, American Whitcomb Judson invented a sliding device with interlocking teeth that he used for fastening boots. Unfortunately, his device tended to jam or burst open. In 1914, Gideon Sundback made the first zip fastener to be used for clothing.

Tape for attaching zip to garment

Teeth lock together

Slide forces teeth together and apart

Handle

EARLY ZIP FASTENER

Waterproof fabric

IN THE RAIN
Collapsible umbrellas were in use before 1800, but were very heavy. In 1848 Samuel Fox introduced steel frames, which were much lighter.

BLUE JEANS

Copper rivets reinforce seams

Jeans were first made in 1874 by Jacob Davis and Levi Strauss. They were designed for gold miners, who complained that their ordinary trousers wore out too quickly.

Rubber-coated fabric

STAYING DRY

Thanks to Charles Macintosh, whose method of waterproofing fabric has been applied to boots as well as coats, it is possible to walk through puddles without getting wet feet.

Strong seam

Jeans are made of denim, a tough cotton fabric.

Moulded rubber sole

LYCRA

Introduced in 1959, Lycra was originally intended for underwear. Its figure-hugging qualities make it ideal for all kinds of clothing, from swimwear to socks.

Lycra is light and stretchy.

LYCRA LEGGINGS

CLOTHING FACTS

• The ancient Romans developed shoes fitted for left and right feet.

• Bloomers were introduced in America in 1851 by women's rights campaigner, Amelia Bloomer.

• Velcro was patented in 1956 by Georges de Mestral of Switzerland, who was fed up with zips that kept jamming.

HYGIENE AND HEALTH

KEEPING CLEAN NOT ONLY MAKES life more pleasant for ourselves and our companions, but also helps to discourage infection and disease. Clean water and good sanitation are essential for healthy living, while drugs and medicines can both prevent and fight infections and illness.

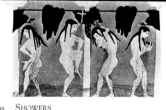

CLEAN WATER

In 1804, Scotsman John Gibb built a filter, like the one shown below, that was large enough to supply the whole city of Paisley in Scotland with clean water. As rainwater flowed through the layers of sand, gravel, and stones, the impurities in the water were filtered out.

SHOWERS

The first showers are thought to date back to 1350 B.C. This Greek vase painting from about 600 B.C. shows a communal shower that appears to have nozzles for the water.

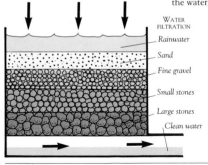

WATER
FILTRATION

Rainwater

Sand

Fine gravel

Small stones

Large stones

Clean water

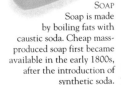

SOAP

Soap is made by boiling fats with caustic soda. Cheap mass-produced soap first became available in the early 1800s, after the introduction of synthetic soda.

HEALTH FACTS

• All drugs were given orally until 1853, when C. Pravaz invented the hypodermic syringe.

• Toilet paper was invented in 1857.

• In 1945, Fleming, Chain, and Florey were awarded the Nobel prize for medicine, for their work on penicillin.

PREVENTING DISEASE

Vaccines enable people to develop immunity to diseases. The first successful vaccine, which prevented smallpox, was produced in 1796 by Edward Jenner.

Cistern holds water that flushes waste down toilet

Plunger

SYRINGE
(1850s)

Cylinder holds vaccine to be injected

Water travels down pipe to bowl

Handle

FIGHTING INFECTION

In 1928, Alexander Fleming discovered penicillin, a mould that could kill bacteria and was to revolutionize the treatment of infections. The drug was developed for medical use by Ernst Chain and Howard Florey.

PENICILLIN
TABLETS
(1951)

Needle

10 TROCHES
PENIGUM
(SUGAR-COATED)
PENICILLIN CHEWING TROCHES

FLUSHING AWAY

The flushing toilet was invented by poet John Harington in 1596. But it wasn't until the 1850s, when a few homes had running water and drains, that the invention caught on.

U-bend prevents backflow of waste

FLUSHING TOILET
(19TH CENTURY)

Bowl

KEEPING TIME

BEFORE PENDULUM CLOCKS were invented,
people relied on the position of the sun
to tell the time. They also invented
sandglasses and other
devices for measuring
fixed periods of time.
Since the 1960s,
mechanical clocks and
watches have been
replaced by electrical
and electronic devices.

SUNDIAL
(1700s)

*Dial marked
off in hours*

Gnomon

PENDULUM CLOCK
In the 1580s, Italian Galileo
Galilei suggested using
the regular swing of a
pendulum to control
a clock. The first
pendulum clock was
made in 1657 by
Dutch scientist
Christiaan Huygens.

*Each swing of the
pendulum moves
the clock hands
forwards.*

*Weight drives
clock mechanism*

PENDULUM
CLOCK

CASTING A SHADOW
Shadow clocks, the forerunners
of sundials, were used in Egypt
and China about 4,000
years ago. The Arabs
developed more accurate
sundials with sloping
gnomons – rods that cast
a shadow on the dial.

Narrow hole

RUNNING OUT OF TIME
In the 1st century A.D., the
Romans used sandglasses to
keep time. The sand took
a fixed amount of time to
flow through the hole
from the top to the
bottom of the glass.

4 2

Time displayed in digital form

LONGINES electronic

ELECTRONIC CLOCK

Hours | Minutes | Seconds

Knob for winding up spiral spring

POCKET WATCH
(EARLY 1900S)

QUARTZ CLOCK
First made in 1929, quartz clocks have no moving parts but depend on the regular vibrations of a tiny quartz crystal. Electronic circuits inside the clock turn these vibrations into signals that drive a digital display.

The spiral spring winds and unwinds, keeping the balance wheel in motion.

Liquid crystal display

Balance wheel swings to and fro

DIGITAL WATCH
Thanks to microelectronic circuits, or "chips", the workings of a quartz clock can now be squeezed into a wrist watch. Liquid crystal displays were invented in the 1970s.

EARLY WATCH
Eighteen years after inventing the pendulum clock, Huygens devised the spiral balance, which meant that accurate clocks could eventually be made small enough to fit into a pocket.

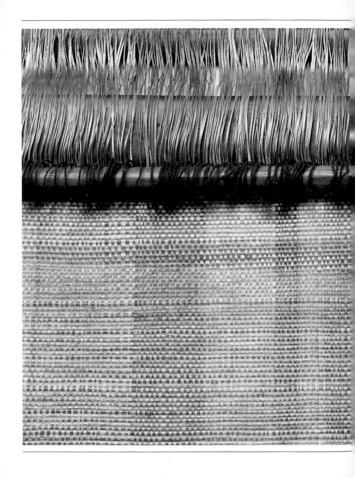

TRADE AND INDUSTRY

INTRODUCTION

INDUSTRY INVOLVES MAKING GOODS or providing services, and trade depends on the ability to buy and sell them. The invention of money, weights, and measures has played an important part in the development of trade, while the ability both to harness energy and make large-scale machinery has enabled industry to flourish.

Wicker purse for carrying shells

INDIAN COWRIE SHELLS

Cowrie shells

Arm with scale

Steelyards were easy to carry and were popular with travelling merchants.

STEELYARD (17TH CENTURY)

Movable weight

MAKING PAYMENTS
Money began as tokens that were exchanged for goods and services. In some prehistoric societies, cowrie shells like these were used as money. Coins and banknotes were invented later.

WEIGHING AND MEASURING
It would be impossible for people to trade without knowing the quantity of the goods changing hands. To prevent arguments about this, people devised various methods of measuring length, volume, and weight.

Hooks on which goods are hung

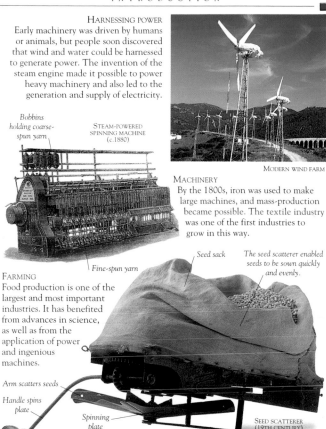

HARNESSING POWER
Early machinery was driven by humans or animals, but people soon discovered that wind and water could be harnessed to generate power. The invention of the steam engine made it possible to power heavy machinery and also led to the generation and supply of electricity.

Bobbins holding coarse-spun yarn

STEAM-POWERED SPINNING MACHINE (c.1880)

Fine-spun yarn

MODERN WIND FARM

MACHINERY
By the 1800s, iron was used to make large machines, and mass-production became possible. The textile industry was one of the first industries to grow in this way.

Seed sack

The seed scatterer enabled seeds to be sown quickly and evenly.

FARMING
Food production is one of the largest and most important industries. It has benefited from advances in science, as well as from the application of power and ingenious machines.

Arm scatters seeds

Handle spins plate

Spinning plate

SEED SCATTERER (19TH CENTURY)

BUYING AND SELLING

BEFORE THE INVENTION of money, people used to trade by barter. In other words, they simply exchanged one item or service for another. Gradually, people began to use tokens, then coins and banknotes to pay for goods. Today, money transactions are often made by computer and do not involve any cash at all.

ROMAN COINS

Roman coins were stamped with the emperor's head.

THE FIRST COINS
Coins were first made in Lydia (now part of Turkey) in the 7th century B.C. and soon spread to other countries of the Mediterranean.

PAYING WITH PAPER
Paper money was first issued on a large scale in the 11th century by the Mongolian emperor, Kubla Khan. European banknotes appeared in 1661.

CHINESE BANKNOTE (1300s)

This note was worth 1,000 coins.

Measuring 22.8 x 33 cm (9 x 13 in), this banknote was the largest ever issued.

■

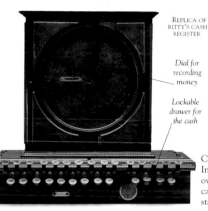

REPLICA OF
RITTY'S CASH
REGISTER

Dial for
recording
money

Lockable
drawer for
the cash

MONEY FACTS

• Milled edging was invented to stop people from filing pieces of metal from coin edges.

• The world's first cash dispensing machine was installed in London in 1967.

• There are about 600 million credit cards in circulation worldwide.

CASH REGISTER
In 1879, American saloon-bar owner James Ritty invented the cash register to stop dishonest staff from stealing cash.

PAYING BY CHEQUE
Cheques are simply signed instructions to banks to pay money directly from one account to another. The first cheque was handled by British bankers Clayton and Morris in 1659.

Bank account
number

Cheque must be
signed here

MODERN CHEQUE

BARCLAYS
HIGH STREET, CAXTON, LONDON, N99 4XX

19

20-99-93
BARCLAYS BANK PLC

only

Pay

SPECIMEN

£

A N OTHER

Cheque No   Branch No   Account No

‡500033‡ 20‑9993‡ 0123456‡

BARCLAYCARD   MasterCard

5301 2500 0123

2182 08/33-03/35

R LATRIM

PLASTIC MONEY
Credit cards enable people to buy goods or services and pay for them later with cash or a cheque. The first credit card was issued in 1950 by the Diner's Club and could be used in any one of 27 restaurants in New York.

WEIGHTS AND MEASURES

SINCE TRADING BEGAN, people have invented different ways of weighing and measuring goods. Initially, people simply used their hands or arms to compare things, but advances in trade demanded more accurate methods. The first systems of weights and measures were devised in ancient times by the Egyptians and the Babylonians.

Horizontal arm
with scale

ROMAN
STEELYARD

GOLD WEIGHTS
(1700s)

Pivot

Weight is
moved along
arm

STANDARD WEIGHTS
These decorative gold weights were made and used by the Ashanti people, who rose to power in Africa during the 18th century.

Scale pan holds
goods to be
weighed

MEASUREMENT FACTS

• An inch was initially measured as the width of the thumb.

• The metric system of measurement was introduced in France in 1795.

• The foot is derived from the Romans, who used a soldier's foot as a unit of length.

BALANCING ACT
Steelyards like this were invented by the Romans and used for weighing out food and crops. The weight was moved along the arm until it balanced with the scale pan. The measurement was then read from the scale.

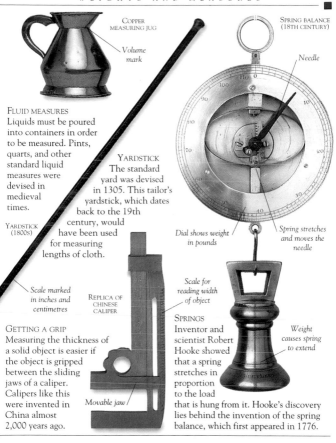

COPPER MEASURING JUG

Volume mark

SPRING BALANCE (18TH CENTURY)

Needle

FLUID MEASURES
Liquids must be poured into containers in order to be measured. Pints, quarts, and other standard liquid measures were devised in medieval times.

YARDSTICK (1800s)

YARDSTICK
The standard yard was devised in 1305. This tailor's yardstick, which dates back to the 19th century, would have been used for measuring lengths of cloth.

Dial shows weight in pounds

Spring stretches and moves the needle

Scale marked in inches and centimetres

REPLICA OF CHINESE CALIPER

Scale for reading width of object

GETTING A GRIP
Measuring the thickness of a solid object is easier if the object is gripped between the sliding jaws of a caliper. Calipers like this were invented in China almost 2,000 years ago.

Movable jaw

SPRINGS
Inventor and scientist Robert Hooke showed that a spring stretches in proportion to the load that is hung from it. Hooke's discovery lies behind the invention of the spring balance, which first appeared in 1776.

Weight causes spring to extend

INDUSTRIAL INVENTIONS

LARGE-SCALE INDUSTRY involves using power and machinery to manufacture goods. Inventions have led to huge changes in industry by providing new sources of power, materials, and manufacturing techniques.

Energy and power

One of the keys to industrial growth was the ability to harness energy. Before the 1700s, most factories depended on wind or water for power. But industry was transformed by the arrival of the steam engine, which could provide power for large factories and mines.

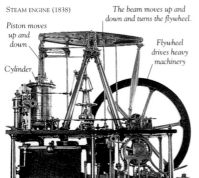

STEAM ENGINE (1838)

The beam moves up and down and turns the flywheel.

Piston moves up and down

Cylinder

Flywheel drives heavy machinery

WATER WHEEL
By 70 B.C., the Romans were using water wheels to grind corn and press olives. Water power was later used to drive heavy machinery in cotton mills and other factories.

THE STEAM ENGINE
Thomas Newcomen invented the steam engine in 1712. Early steam engines were simply used for pumping, but later engines could turn wheels and heavy machinery as well.

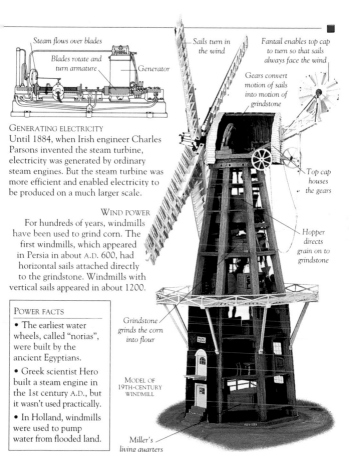

Steam flows over blades

Blades rotate and turn armature

Generator

Sails turn in the wind

Fantail enables top cap to turn so that sails always face the wind

Gears convert motion of sails into motion of grindstone

Top cap houses the gears

Hopper directs grain on to grindstone

GENERATING ELECTRICITY

Until 1884, when Irish engineer Charles Parsons invented the steam turbine, electricity was generated by ordinary steam engines. But the steam turbine was more efficient and enabled electricity to be produced on a much larger scale.

WIND POWER

For hundreds of years, windmills have been used to grind corn. The first windmills, which appeared in Persia in about A.D. 600, had horizontal sails attached directly to the grindstone. Windmills with vertical sails appeared in about 1200.

Grindstone grinds the corn into flour

MODEL OF
19TH-CENTURY
WINDMILL

Miller's living quarters

POWER FACTS

• The earliest water wheels, called "norias", were built by the ancient Egyptians.

• Greek scientist Hero built a steam engine in the 1st century A.D., but it wasn't used practically.

• In Holland, windmills were used to pump water from flooded land.

Spinning and weaving

WOVEN
FABRIC

People started to make cloth about 10,000 years ago, using simple machines to spin and weave the yarn. The arrival of spinning wheels and looms meant that cloth could be made much more quickly, but it wasn't until the 1800s, when spinning and weaving became fully mechanized, that the textile industry began to flourish.

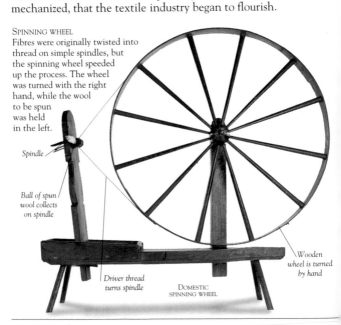

SPINNING WHEEL
Fibres were originally twisted into thread on simple spindles, but the spinning wheel speeded up the process. The wheel was turned with the right hand, while the wool to be spun was held in the left.

Spindle

Ball of spun wool collects on spindle

Driver thread turns spindle

DOMESTIC SPINNING WHEEL

Wooden wheel is turned by hand

JACQUARD LOOM
(EARLY 1800S)

Punched cards
programme the
loom to weave
patterns.

THE COTTON GIN
Before cotton can be spun, the fibre
must be removed from the seeds. This
used to be a tedious task, but in 1792
American Eli Whitney invented the
cotton gin, which did the job in a
fraction of the time.

PATTERNED FABRICS
Weaving patterns was hard
until 1805, when Joseph-
Marie Jacquard devised a
programmable loom. The
loom was controlled by
punched cards, on which
the designs were stored.

Raw
cotton

Seedless cotton
collects here

MODEL OF COTTON GIN
(1792)

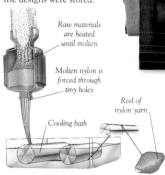

Raw materials
are heated
until molten

Molten nylon is
forced through
tiny holes

Cooling bath

Reel of
nylon yarn

NYLON SPINNING
Nylon plastic was first spun into yarn
in the late 1930s. The process involves
forcing molten nylon through tiny holes
so that it solidifies into slender fibres.
The fibres are then spun into a single
thread and wound onto a reel.

Metalworking

Metals are so important that two periods in history, the Bronze Age and the Iron Age, have been named after them. The large-scale production of iron made it possible to build heavy machinery and was vital for industrial development.

WORKING WITH BRONZE

Bronze is a mixture of tin and copper and was first made in about 3500 B.C. It was melted down and cast into different shapes. Once set, it was strong and did not corrode, so it was ideal for making swords and daggers.

ALUMINIUM FOOD WRAP

ALUMINIUM

Aluminium, the most common metal on Earth, was discovered in 1825 by Danish scientist Hans Oersted. Light and easily shaped, it is made into all kinds of things, from food wrap to aeroplanes.

ROMAN IRON NAILS (A.D. 88)

Edges could be resharpened

Early iron objects were hammered into shape.

BRONZE SWORD

HARD AS NAILS

When it is heated, iron softens enough to be hammered into shape. From 1500 B.C., iron was used in this way to make nails and other objects.

METAL FACTS

• The Greeks and Romans made mirrors from polished bronze.

• In prehistoric times, people extracted iron from meteors that fell from the sky.

• Mercury is liquid at room temperature and is used in thermometers and tooth fillings.

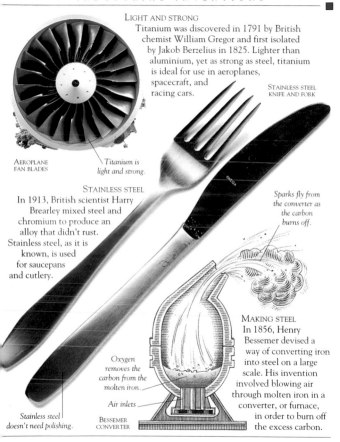

LIGHT AND STRONG

Titanium was discovered in 1791 by British chemist William Gregor and first isolated by Jakob Berzelius in 1825. Lighter than aluminium, yet as strong as steel, titanium is ideal for use in aeroplanes, spacecraft, and racing cars.

STAINLESS STEEL KNIFE AND FORK

AEROPLANE FAN BLADES

Titanium is light and strong.

STAINLESS STEEL

In 1913, British scientist Harry Brearley mixed steel and chromium to produce an alloy that didn't rust. Stainless steel, as it is known, is used for saucepans and cutlery.

Sparks fly from the converter as the carbon burns off.

MAKING STEEL

In 1856, Henry Bessemer devised a way of converting iron into steel on a large scale. His invention involved blowing air through molten iron in a converter, or furnace, in order to burn off the excess carbon.

Oxygen removes the carbon from the molten iron.

Air inlets

BESSEMER CONVERTER

Stainless steel doesn't need polishing.

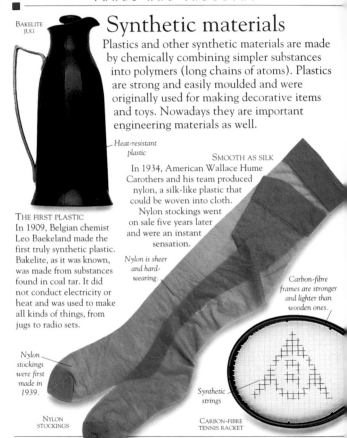

BAKELITE
JUG

Synthetic materials

Plastics and other synthetic materials are made
by chemically combining simpler substances
into polymers (long chains of atoms). Plastics
are strong and easily moulded and were
originally used for making decorative items
and toys. Nowadays they are important
engineering materials as well.

*Heat-resistant
plastic*

SMOOTH AS SILK
In 1934, American Wallace Hume
Carothers and his team produced
nylon, a silk-like plastic that
could be woven into cloth.
Nylon stockings went
on sale five years later
and were an instant
sensation.

THE FIRST PLASTIC
In 1909, Belgian chemist
Leo Baekeland made the
first truly synthetic plastic.
Bakelite, as it was known,
was made from substances
found in coal tar. It did
not conduct electricity or
heat and was used to make
all kinds of things, from
jugs to radio sets.

*Nylon is sheer
and hard-
wearing.*

*Carbon-fibre
frames are stronger
and lighter than
wooden ones.*

*Nylon
stockings
were first
made in
1939.*

*Synthetic
strings*

NYLON
STOCKINGS

CARBON-FIBRE
TENNIS RACKET

SYNTHETIC RUBBER
The first synthetic rubber gloves, made in 1952, were intended for surgical and industrial use. Household rubber gloves were launched by the London Rubber Company in 1961.

CELLULOID EVENING BAG (1900)

Clasp

Plaited leather strap

Leather tassle

Moulded celluloid resembles intricately carved ivory.

Raised pattern increases grip

HOUSEHOLD RUBBER GLOVES

IVORY SUBSTITUTE
Celluloid is a semi-synthetic plastic made from cellulose, a plant fibre. First produced in 1869 by John Wesley Hyatt, celluloid was used to make roll-films for cameras as well as imitation ivory items like this evening bag.

POLYTHENE
Discovered accidentally by British scientist R. Gibson in 1933, polythene is a tough, waterproof plastic, ideal for making food containers.

FOOD CONTAINERS

Handle

COMPOSITES
Plastics can be combined with carbon fibres to make composite materials that are both light and strong.

Mass-production

When goods are manufactured in large quantities, they are cheaper to produce, and more people can afford to buy them. The invention of the assembly line, interchangeable part manufacture, and other time-saving devices have all helped to make mass-production possible.

Steering wheel

FORD MODEL T
(1913)

Openable windscreen

Mass-produced Model Ts were available only in black.

DRILL BIT
In 1865, F. W. Taylor devised a special steel that could withstand heavy use. Drill bits made from this steel were ideal for mass-production because they could be used again and again without going blunt.

Side lamp

Radiator

Horn

Headlamp

Starting handle

Wooden-spoked wheel

ASSEMBLY LINE
The Ford Model T was the first car to be built on a moving assembly line. Cars moved along a conveyer, and each worker fitted just one part, cutting the time taken to build a car from 12 hours to less than 2 hours.

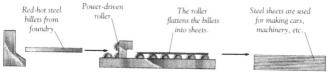

Red-hot steel billets from foundry

Power-driven roller

The roller flattens the billets into sheets.

Steel sheets are used for making cars, machinery, etc.

ROLLING MILL

First built in 1926, large-scale rolling mills were vital for the growth of modern industry. Rolling mills supply factories with steel rolled into sheets, rods, or bars of uniform thickness and quality.

WELDING

In 1890, Russian Nikolai Slavyanov invented electric arc welding, a quick and easy way of joining metals. An electric current creates a spot of heat on the metal so that the two pieces of metal fuse.

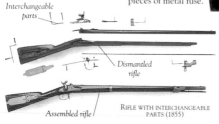

Interchangeable parts

Dismantled rifle

Assembled rifle

RIFLE WITH INTERCHANGEABLE PARTS (1855)

INTERCHANGEABLE PARTS

Developed in the 1800s, interchangeable parts were used widely in the manufacture of rifles. The parts could be fitted easily into any rifle, saving precious minutes on the assembly line.

UNTOUCHED BY HUMAN HANDS

Since the 1970s, robots have been used to replace human workers on production lines. The first robots could only move things from one place to another, but robots can now reproduce a range of human movements, without getting tired.

ARTS AND CRAFTS

MANY OF TODAY'S CRAFTS originated hundreds, or even thousands, of years ago and depend on simple inventions that were revolutionary in their time. These crafts have been kept alive because many people still value handmade products in an age when most things are made by machine.

POTTER'S WHEEL

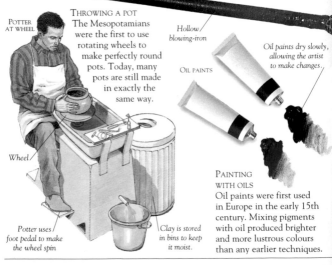

POTTER AT WHEEL

THROWING A POT
The Mesopotamians were the first to use rotating wheels to make perfectly round pots. Today, many pots are still made in exactly the same way.

Wheel

Potter uses foot pedal to make the wheel spin.

Clay is stored in bins to keep it moist.

Hollow blowing-iron

OIL PAINTS

Oil paints dry slowly, allowing the artist to make changes.

PAINTING
WITH OILS
Oil paints were first used in Europe in the early 15th century. Mixing pigments with oil produced brighter and more lustrous colours than any earlier techniques.

KNITTING
The earliest evidence of knitting is the remains of an Arabian sock that dates back to 700 B.C. Despite the invention of knitting machines, hand-knitting is still a popular pastime.

Knitting needles

Wool

Lace

Bobbin

Cotton thread

Glass is blown into a bulb shape

Beads weigh bobbin down to keep thread straight

LACE-MAKING
The art of lace-making originated in France and Belgium during the 14th century. Long needles, or bobbins, are plaited over and under each other to create intricate patterns in the lace.

Molten glass falls into mould

Mould is used to measure out correct quantity of glass

Strong shears

GLASS-BLOWING
In about 100 B.C., Syrian glassworkers found that a blob of molten glass on the end of a pipe could be blown into a bulb. This technique was used to make goblets and other items, and is still used today to make hand-crafted glassware.

FARMING

BEFORE THE GROWTH OF INDUSTRY, most people worked on the land and produced their own food. But as people moved to the cities to work, they began to rely on the remaining farmers to supply them with food. Inventions that enabled farmers to produce more crops with less labour became widely used.

PREHISTORIC
FARMING
TOOLS

Cultivating the land

The development of pest control and artificial fertilizers meant that crops could be grown more abundantly. Labour-saving devices were then needed to ease the tasks of working the soil and harvesting. With the arrival of iron and steel, and the invention of the internal combustion engine, land farming soon became mechanized.

Handle is turned to lift water

Water

LIFTING WATER
In about 236 B.C., Greek inventor Archimedes gave his name to a screw pump, which used the principle of the inclined plane to lift water. The pump was later used for raising water from low-lying rivers and canals in order to water crops on higher land.

Water moves up tube

End of plough was attached to a team of horses or oxen

WOODEN
PLOUGH (1763)

Coulter slices a furrow in the ground

COMBINE HARVESTER

In 1838, Americans J. Hascall and Hiram Moore built a machine that could cut the crop and put the grain into sacks. Their machine was so large that it needed more than 30 mules to pull it. The first self-propelled "combine" appeared in 1910.

Threshing cylinder separates the grain from the heads

Auger unloads the grain

Cutter slices crop stalks

Conveyor carries stalks to threshing cylinder

MODERN COMBINE HARVESTER

CROP-DUSTING

Applying fertilizers and pesticides to huge fields can be very time-consuming, so it makes sense to spray them from low-flying aeroplanes. This was first done in the U.S.A. in 1925.

Mouldboard lifts and turns the soil

MODEL OF McCORMICK'S REAPER

Horse was attached here

Handles allow farmer to control the depth and direction of the cut

Stalks tied into sheaves here

THE PLOUGH

The plough was one of the most important innovations in agriculture. It appeared in Mesopotamia in 3500 B.C. The addition of wheels in the 10th century made the plough easier to control.

Cutter bar

REAPING MACHINE

In 1834, American Cyrus McCormick devised a horse-drawn reaping machine that could both cut the grain and tie it into sheaves. In 1851, McCormick's invention won him a medal at the Great Exhibition in London.

Animal farming and fishing

Rearing animals and catching fish demand a great deal of time and effort. From the automatic milking machine to the power-driven sheep shearer, time-saving gadgets and machinery or inventions that make farming easier have been vital for making both animal farming and fishing more profitable.

HYDRAULIC COW MILKER (1868)

MILKING MACHINE
Powered milking machines appeared in the 1880s but, like earlier hand-operated machines, they were painful for the cows. In 1895, Scotsman Alexander Shields made a gentler machine that used a pulsating vacuum to mimic a suckling calf.

SHEARING SHEEP
One of the first sets of power-driven wool clippers was made by Frederick Wolseley in 1868. Wolseley later became famous as a car maker, with his partner Herbert Austin.

BARBED WIRE
The use of barbed wire to fence off areas of land made cattle farming much less labour-intensive and put many cowboys out of work. Barbed wire was patented by American farmer Joseph Glidden in 1874.

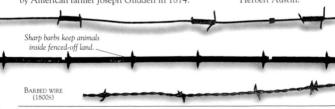

Sharp barbs keep animals inside fenced-off land.

BARBED WIRE (1800s)

*The ancient
Egyptians made
nets from reed and papyrus.*

CASTING NETS

The first fishing nets, which
appeared before 6500 B.C., were
made by knotting together lengths
of papyrus or yarn. Net-making
machinery was introduced
during the late 1800s, and
by the 1960s, fishing nets
were being made from
synthetic fibres.

FISH HOOKS

The discovery of copper and bronze
meant that metal fish hooks could be
made and used for fishing on a
smaller scale than with nets.
The cunning addition
of the barb, which
trapped the fish
once it had bitten,
appeared in about
3000 B.C.

*Hook
attaches to
fishing line*

*Winches haul
up heavy
catches.*

MODERN
FISHING BOAT

EARLY FISH
HOOKS

*Barbed
end*

TRAWLING FOR FISH

Large-scale fishing took
off in the 1880s, when steam
engines were fitted to fishing boats.
The boats dragged nets through the
water behind them, sweeping up larger
catches than ever before.

*Fish are
trapped in
the net.*

SCIENCE AND COMMUNICATION

SCIENCE AND COMMUNICATION

INTRODUCTION

INVENTION AND SCIENTIFIC DISCOVERY often go hand in hand. Discoveries can lead to important inventions, while inventions can give scientists the means to both confirm their theories and make new discoveries.

ELECTRONIC
CALCULATOR

Keypad

BEYOND VISION
Optical inventions such as microscopes and telescopes led to advances in astronomy and biology, allowing scientists to see things that they had never seen before, from distant galaxies to tiny micro-organisms.

MICROSCOPE
(1728)

ADDING UP
Many devices, from abacuses to electronic calculators, have been invented to help with counting and computing.

UNDERSTANDING THE WEATHER
Barometers, thermometers, and other weather-measuring instruments have enabled scientists to learn more about the climate and to predict weather patterns.

Lens focuses light

Stage holds specimen

Tilting mirror

Pointer indicates air pressure

ANEROID
BAROMETER

MEDICINE AND SURGERY
Advances in biology and chemistry have helped scientists to gain a better understanding of the human body and its diseases. Developments in technology have helped them to diagnose and treat those diseases.

Valves

PLUG-IN PANEL
FROM COMPUTER
(1950s)

Pelvic socket

MODERN
ARTIFICIAL
HIP JOINT

Metal stem fits into leg bone

ELECTRICITY AND ELECTRONICS
From light bulbs to computers, many of the things that we use today are powered by electricity or controlled by electronics.

Hook for earpiece

Mouthpiece converts sound into electrical signals

COMMUNICATION
Information has become one of the most important commodities in modern life. Inventions such as the telephone and the fax machine have helped to speed information across the globe in an instant.

Earpiece converts electrical signals into sound

Wire

Numbered dial connects caller

DIAL TELEPHONE
(c.1929)

COUNTING AND COMPUTING

DEVICES THAT AID COUNTING have been around
for thousands of years. About 5,000 years ago, the
Mesopotamians recorded their
calculations by sliding small stones
along furrows in the ground – an
idea similar to the abacus,
which appeared
later in China
and Japan.

*Upper beads
represent five
times the value
of lower beads.*

ABACUS
Although it is the oldest calculating
device, the abacus is still in use
today. Numbers are recorded
by moving the beads,
which are arranged in
rows representing
units, tens, etc.

*Scales are used
to multiply
numbers.*

SLIDE RULE

SLIDE RULE
Englishman
William Oughtred
invented the slide
rule in about 1622. His
device used John Napier's
invention of logarithms,
which transformed the tedious
task of multiplication into addition.

BABBAGE'S
DIFFERENCE
ENGINE (1832)

BABBAGE'S ENGINE
This machine, built
in 1832 by Charles
Babbage, was the
first automatic
calculator. Babbage
went on to design
a programmable
machine, which
unfortunately
was never
built.

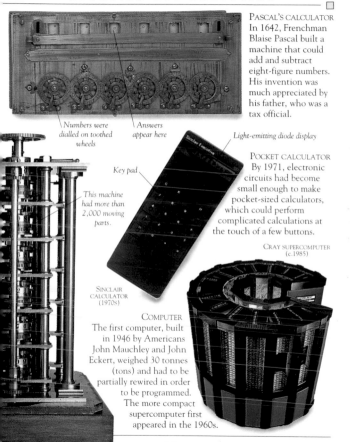

PASCAL'S CALCULATOR
In 1642, Frenchman
Blaise Pascal built a
machine that could
add and subtract
eight-figure numbers.
His invention was
much appreciated by
his father, who was a
tax official.

*Numbers were
dialled on toothed
wheels*

*Answers
appear here*

Light-emitting diode display

POCKET CALCULATOR
By 1971, electronic
circuits had become
small enough to make
pocket-sized calculators,
which could perform
complicated calculations at
the touch of a few buttons.

Key pad

*This machine
had more than
2,000 moving
parts.*

CRAY SUPERCOMPUTER
(c.1985)

SINCLAIR
CALCULATOR
(1970s)

COMPUTER
The first computer, built
in 1946 by Americans
John Mauchley and John
Eckert, weighed 30 tonnes
(tons) and had to be
partially rewired in order
to be programmed.
The more compact
supercomputer first
appeared in the 1960s.

OPTICAL INVENTIONS

MICROSCOPES, TELESCOPES, and other optical inventions have been vital for advances in science. Most optical devices contain lenses, which can make small objects appear larger or distant objects appear closer. Lenses depend on the fact that rays of light bend, or refract, as they pass from air to glass.

Observer looks here

Sliding focus

WATCHING THE STARS

The first telescope was built in 1608 by Dutchman Hans Lippershey. It had two lenses that refracted the light and made distant objects look much closer. A year later, Italian Galileo Galilei used a similar telescope to study the Moon.

Telescope swivels on wooden ball

NEWTON'S REFLECTOR (1668)

GALILEO'S TELESCOPE (EARLY 17TH CENTURY)

MAGNIFYING WITH MIRRORS

In 1668, Isaac Newton built the first reflecting telescope, which used curved mirrors instead of lenses to magnify distant objects. Newton's reflector produced much clearer images than refracting telescopes of the time.

MAGNIFYING GLASS

Robert Grosseteste was the first to suggest using lenses to magnify small objects. His pupil, Roger Bacon, made the first magnifying glass in 1267.

MAGNIFYING GLASS
(17TH CENTURY)

Coloured glass

Lens

Ribbons were attached here

Lens holder

IRON-FRAMED SPECTACLES
(1750)

SPECTACLES

Made in Venice in about 1280, the first spectacles had convex (outward-curving) lenses and were suitable only for close-up vision.

MICROSCOPE

The first compound microscope (with two or more lenses) was made in 1590 by Hans Janssen and his son, Zacharias. It enabled them to see tiny objects, invisible to the naked eye.

Eyepiece lens

Lens focuses light on to stage

Objective lens

Stage for holding specimen

Focusing screw

Mirror reflects light from lamp or window

COMPOUND MICROSCOPE
(1767)

Eyepiece lens

Prisms reflect the light back on itself, lengthening its path.

SEEING DOUBLE?

Binoculars use prisms (specially shaped blocks of glass) to reflect the light. Because the prisms send the light backwards and forwards, binoculars can be made much shorter than telescopes. The first "prismatic" binoculars were made in about 1880.

OPTICAL FACTS

• People thought the Moon was smooth until Galileo saw its craters through his telescope.

• Bifocal spectacles were invented in 1784 by Benjamin Franklin.

• Microscopic cells were first described by Robert Hooke in 1665.

RECORDING THE WEATHER

METEOROLOGY, THE SCIENTIFIC study of the weather, began in Italy during the 17th century, when scientists started to devise instruments that could measure changes in the temperature, pressure, and moisture content of the air. Records about the weather could then be used to note patterns and make forecasts.

THERMOMETER (18TH CENTURY)

Scale shows temperature

Mercury bulb

THERMOMETER
The mercury thermometer was devised by Gabriel Fahrenheit in 1714. As the air temperature rises, the mercury in the bulb expands and moves up the glass tube.

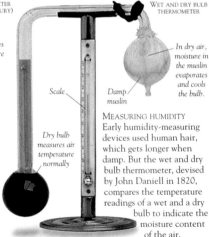

WET AND DRY BULB THERMOMETER

In dry air, moisture in the muslin evaporates and cools the bulb.

Damp muslin

Scale

Dry bulb measures air temperature normally

MEASURING HUMIDITY
Early humidity-measuring devices used human hair, which gets longer when damp. But the wet and dry bulb thermometer, devised by John Daniell in 1820, compares the temperature readings of a wet and a dry bulb to indicate the moisture content of the air.

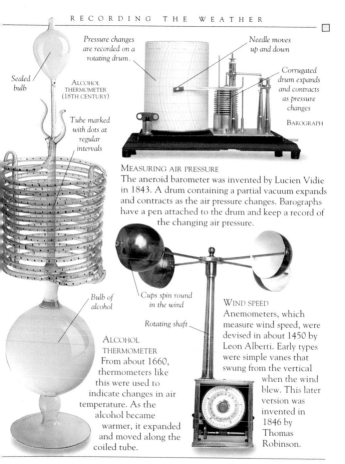

Pressure changes are recorded on a rotating drum.

Needle moves up and down

Sealed bulb

ALCOHOL THERMOMETER (18TH CENTURY)

Corrugated drum expands and contracts as pressure changes

BAROGRAPH

Tube marked with dots at regular intervals

MEASURING AIR PRESSURE

The aneroid barometer was invented by Lucien Vidie in 1843. A drum containing a partial vacuum expands and contracts as the air pressure changes. Barographs have a pen attached to the drum and keep a record of the changing air pressure.

Cups spin round in the wind

Bulb of alcohol

Rotating shaft

WIND SPEED

Anemometers, which measure wind speed, were devised in about 1450 by Leon Alberti. Early types were simple vanes that swung from the vertical when the wind blew. This later version was invented in 1846 by Thomas Robinson.

ALCOHOL THERMOMETER

From about 1660, thermometers like this were used to indicate changes in air temperature. As the alcohol became warmer, it expanded and moved along the coiled tube.

ELECTRICITY

IN 1752, AFTER FLYING his kite in a thunderstorm, American scientist Benjamin Franklin showed that lightning was a form of electricity. Franklin's work led to a huge interest in electrical science and paved the way for many new and exciting inventions and discoveries.

Glass rod

Zinc disc

Copper disc

LIGHTNING ROD (1750S)

Lightning rod discharges electricity into the ground

Rod was attached to the highest point of building

THE FIRST BATTERY
In 1800, Italian scientist Alessandro Volta made the first battery by piling up alternate copper and zinc discs separated by cloth pads soaked in weak acid. An electrochemical reaction between the discs generated a constant flow of electric charge.

Cloth pad soaked in salt water or weak acid

VOLTAIC PILE

Wooden base

LIGHTNING ROD
Franklin's experiments led him to invent the lightning rod in 1752. The rod was attached to the highest point of a building to prevent the building from being struck by lightning during thunderstorms.

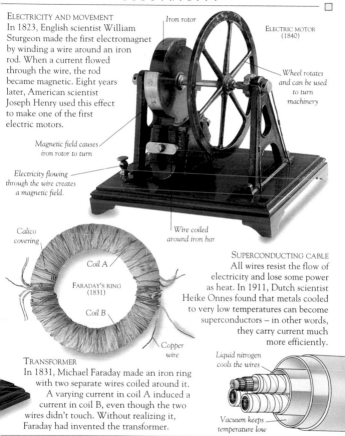

ELECTRICITY AND MOVEMENT

In 1823, English scientist William Sturgeon made the first electromagnet by winding a wire around an iron rod. When a current flowed through the wire, the rod became magnetic. Eight years later, American scientist Joseph Henry used this effect to make one of the first electric motors.

Iron rotor

ELECTRIC MOTOR (1840)

Wheel rotates and can be used to turn machinery

Magnetic field causes iron rotor to turn

Electricity flowing through the wire creates a magnetic field.

Wire coiled around iron bar

Calico covering

Coil A

FARADAY'S RING (1831)

Coil B

Copper wire

SUPERCONDUCTING CABLE

All wires resist the flow of electricity and lose some power as heat. In 1911, Dutch scientist Heike Onnes found that metals cooled to very low temperatures can become superconductors – in other words, they can carry current much more efficiently.

Liquid nitrogen cools the wires

Vacuum keeps temperature low

TRANSFORMER

In 1831, Michael Faraday made an iron ring with two separate wires coiled around it. A varying current in coil A induced a current in coil B, even though the two wires didn't touch. Without realizing it, Faraday had invented the transformer.

ELECTRONICS

TELEVISIONS, COMPUTERS, and many other gadgets that we use today are electronic. Electronics involves using special components to control electricity itself. Over the years, electronic components have become smaller and smaller so that today, millions of electronic circuits can be fitted into a tiny silicon chip.

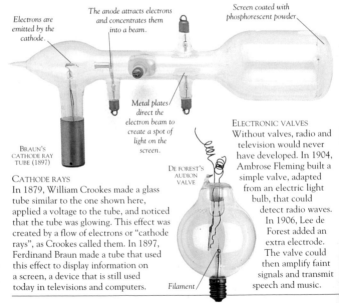

Electrons are emitted by the cathode.

The anode attracts electrons and concentrates them into a beam.

Screen coated with phosphorescent powder

Metal plates direct the electron beam to create a spot of light on the screen.

BRAUN'S CATHODE RAY TUBE (1897)

DE FOREST'S AUDION VALVE

Filament

CATHODE RAYS

In 1879, William Crookes made a glass tube similar to the one shown here, applied a voltage to the tube, and noticed that the tube was glowing. This effect was created by a flow of electrons or "cathode rays", as Crookes called them. In 1897, Ferdinand Braun made a tube that used this effect to display information on a screen, a device that is still used today in televisions and computers.

ELECTRONIC VALVES

Without valves, radio and television would never have developed. In 1904, Ambrose Fleming built a simple valve, adapted from an electric light bulb, that could detect radio waves. In 1906, Lee de Forest added an extra electrode. The valve could then amplify faint signals and transmit speech and music.

Supporting frame

Spring

Probe

EARLY TRANSISTOR

THE FIRST TRANSISTOR

A major breakthrough in electronics came with the invention of the transistor, which did the same job as the valve but was much smaller. Developed by American William Shockley and his team in 1947, the transistor was used in radios and other electronic devices, making them much more compact.

PRINTING A CIRCUIT

Electronic equipment had to be built laboriously by hand until German engineer Paul Eisler came up with the idea of printing the tiny circuits on to copper foil attached to plastic boards. Eisler patented the printed circuit board in 1943. Integrated circuits, or microchips, appeared 16 years later.

Microchip

Tracks connecting components

CIRCUIT BOARD FROM SMALL COMPUTER

RUBY LASER (1960s)

Laser beam

Rod of synthetic ruby

High-intensity lamp

LASERS

In 1960, Theodore Maiman made the first laser. He put a flash tube around a rod of ruby and produced a beam of laser light. Today lasers are used in all kinds of electronic devices, from supermarket scanners to compact disc players.

HEALTH AND MEDICINE

DEVELOPMENTS IN SCIENCE and technology have led
to many advances in health and medicine. Science
allows researchers to unravel the workings of
the human body, while technology
provides the tools with which
doctors can treat their patients.

Surgical inventions

Until the 19th century, surgical
operations were often more life-
threatening than the conditions
they were supposed to cure. But
techniques advanced rapidly during
the 1800s, and the development of
anaesthetics, antiseptics, and new
surgical tools meant that having
an operation became a safer and
less harrowing experience.

Rubber tube

*Valve lets ether
vapour into
rubber tube*

*Valve draws
air into the jar*

*Sponges soaked
in ether*

THE "LETHEON"
ETHER INHALER
(1847)

*Winding
key*

HARRINGTON'S
CLOCKWORK
DENTAL DRILL

Drill bit

DRILLING AND FILLING
Englishman George Harrington devised a
clockwork dental drill in 1863. When fully
wound, the drill would keep going for up
to two agonizing minutes.

GERM-FREE SURGERY

Developed by Joseph Lister in the 1860s, antiseptics reduced the risk of infection during surgery. Lister used a steam spray like this to spray the antiseptic around the operation site.

CARBOLIC STEAM SPRAY (1875)

Mouthpiece

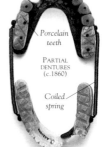

Porcelain teeth

PARTIAL DENTURES (c.1860)

Coiled spring

ANAESTHETICS

In 1846, surgeons began to use ether and chloroform to make their patients unconscious before surgery. The inhaler ensured that only the patient was affected by the anaesthetic.

FALSE TEETH

In 1774, Frenchman Alexis Duchâteau devised the first well-fitting set of false teeth. His partner added springs, which kept the false teeth in place.

SURGICAL FACTS

• In prehistoric times, holes were drilled in people's skulls as a treatment for insanity.

• In about 700 B.C., the Etruscan people of Italy wore dentures that were made from animal teeth.

• During the Middle Ages, surgery was often performed by barbers.

Wire to heart

Pulse generator

SETTING THE PACE

In 1952, American doctor Paul Zoll used electrical impulses to revive a failing heart. This led to the invention of the pacemaker, which is inserted next to the patient's heart and automatically ensures a regular beat.

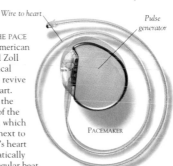

PACEMAKER

Investigative medicine

Surgery can be risky and expensive, so it is important for doctors to be able to find out what is going on inside a patient's body without operating. Investigative techniques are quicker and less painful than surgery and can be used as part of a patient's treatment as well as for checking general health.

NURSING THE SICK

FEELING FEVERISH?
A body temperature just one or two degrees above normal is a sure sign that something is wrong. Thanks to the clinical thermometer, developed by Thomas Allbut in 1866, people can take their own temperature without calling out a doctor.

Temperature scale

Curved thermometer is placed under patient's armpit

Mercury bulb

THERMOMETERS
(c.1865)

Funnel concentrates the light

Candle provides light

Speculum is placed in patient's ear

ENDOSCOPE
(1880s)

Viewing lenses

LOOKING INSIDE
Nineteenth-century physicians used gadgets like this to look inside patients' ears and other awkward places. The modern, flexible endoscope, first made by American Basil Hirschovitz in 1957, uses optical fibres to reach farther with less discomfort.

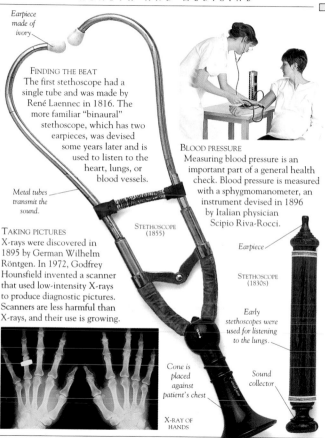

Earpiece made of ivory.

FINDING THE BEAT
The first stethoscope had a single tube and was made by René Laennec in 1816. The more familiar "binaural" stethoscope, which has two earpieces, was devised some years later and is used to listen to the heart, lungs, or blood vessels.

Metal tubes transmit the sound.

STETHOSCOPE (1855)

BLOOD PRESSURE
Measuring blood pressure is an important part of a general health check. Blood pressure is measured with a sphygmomanometer, an instrument devised in 1896 by Italian physician Scipio Riva-Rocci.

Earpiece

STETHOSCOPE (1830s)

Early stethoscopes were used for listening to the lungs.

TAKING PICTURES
X-rays were discovered in 1895 by German Wilhelm Röntgen. In 1972, Godfrey Hounsfield invented a scanner that used low-intensity X-rays to produce diagnostic pictures. Scanners are less harmful than X-rays, and their use is growing.

Cone is placed against patient's chest

Sound collector

X-RAY OF HANDS

85

COMMUNICATION

THE ABILITY TO COMMUNICATE is essential to our everyday lives. Early people conveyed information by word of mouth or by signalling to each other with fires or lights. But as civilizations developed, many new and ingenious ways of passing on information were invented.

Writing

Writing is one of the oldest forms of communication. The first written signs may have developed as a way for traders to keep records of their transactions. Early writing was inscribed on clay or stone using flints and sticks. Paper, inks, and an array of writing implements developed later.

EARLY WRITING
Cuneiform, the first true system of writing, was devised in Mesopotamia more than 5,000 years ago. The wedge-shaped symbols were pressed into wet clay with sharpened sticks.

Papyrus was hammered into sheets.

Reed pens were cut to form a point.

PAPYRUS AND
REED PENS

PAPYRUS
The ancient Egyptians invented papyrus, a form of paper made from pulped reeds, or plant stems. They wrote on the papyrus with reed pens and ink made from water, soot, and natural gum.

Sharpened point

Nib

QUILL PEN

Feathers were first used as pens in around 500 B.C. Because of the way they curve, left wing feathers proved to be more suitable for right-handed people, and vice-versa.

FEATHER QUILL

Feathers from large birds have wide shafts that are easy to hold.

FOUNTAIN PEN

The fountain pen made it possible to write without constantly re-inking the pen. Ink is held in a reservoir inside the pen and flows through the nib to the paper.

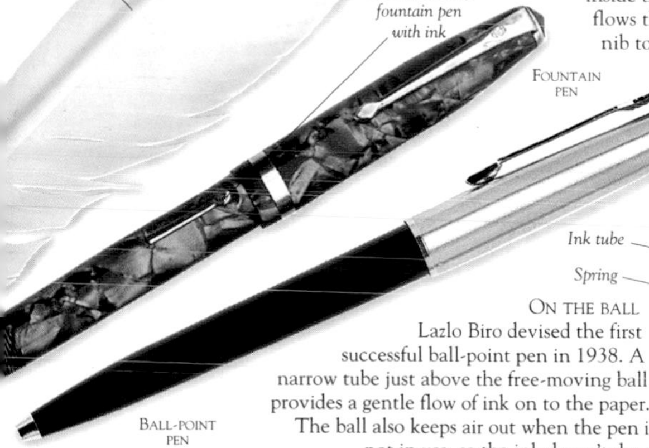

Hollow shaft, or quill

Lever for filling fountain pen with ink

FOUNTAIN PEN

Ink tube

Spring

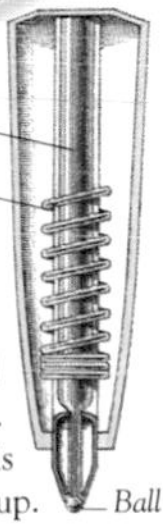

ON THE BALL

Lazlo Biro devised the first successful ball-point pen in 1938. A narrow tube just above the free-moving ball provides a gentle flow of ink on to the paper. The ball also keeps air out when the pen is not in use, so the ink doesn't dry up.

Ball

BALL-POINT PEN

Printing

Before printing, every book had to be written out by hand. This meant that books were rare and expensive, and available only to wealthy people. One of the pioneers of printing was the German Johannes Gutenberg, whose ingenuity enabled books to be produced in large numbers for the first time.

THE FIRST PRINTERS

Book-printing began during the 6th century in Japan and China, where hand-carved wooden blocks were used to print individual pages. A steady hand was essential; one mistake meant the whole block would have to be carved again.

JAPANESE WOODEN PRINTING BLOCK

HAND PRESS
(17TH CENTURY)

TYPECASTING

In 1450, Gutenberg invented movable type – single letters that could be set in lines and re-used. He carved letters to make moulds, poured hot metal into the moulds to make the type, and then set the type on a tray ready for printing.

Hard metal punch used to make mould

Mould used to make piece of type

Tray

Individual pieces of type arranged in reverse

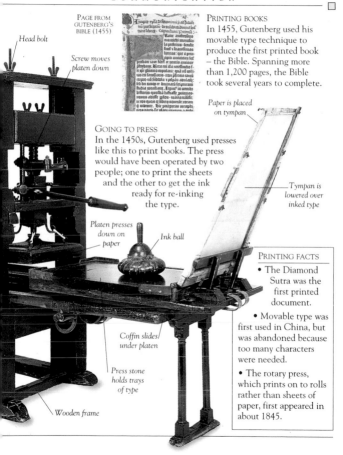

PAGE FROM GUTENBERG'S BIBLE (1455)

PRINTING BOOKS
In 1455, Gutenberg used his movable type technique to produce the first printed book – the Bible. Spanning more than 1,200 pages, the Bible took several years to complete.

Head bolt

Screw moves platen down

Paper is placed on tympan

GOING TO PRESS
In the 1450s, Gutenberg used presses like this to print books. The press would have been operated by two people; one to print the sheets and the other to get the ink ready for re-inking the type.

Tympan is lowered over inked type

Platen presses down on paper

Ink ball

Coffin slides under platen

Press stone holds trays of type

Wooden frame

PRINTING FACTS

• The Diamond Sutra was the first printed document.

• Movable type was first used in China, but was abandoned because too many characters were needed.

• The rotary press, which prints on to rolls rather than sheets of paper, first appeared in about 1845.

Postal services

Before the development of organized postal systems, letters and packages had to be delivered personally or via messengers. The Romans were among the first to have an official mail service, but it wasn't until the 1850s that pre-paid mail could simply be dropped in a postbox and delivered to almost anywhere in the world.

EARLY POSTBOX

POSTING A LETTER

Postboxes save people a trip to the post office. The first postbox was put up in Guernsey in the Channel Islands in 1852. Staff from the local post office collected the mail at regular intervals during the day.

Stamps were invented as proof that the postage has been paid.

POSTAGE STAMPS

POSTAGE STAMPS

People used to pay for their post when it was delivered rather than before it was sent. But Englishman Rowland Hill came up with the idea of paying for postage in advance, and the first postage stamps were introduced in 1840.

ON THE MOVE
The introduction of trains with sorting carriages in 1838 made next-day postal deliveries possible. The post was sorted while the train was on the move.

SENDING GREETINGS
Postcards provide a quick and easy way to send a message. They are thought to have originated during the 1860s in either the U.S.A. or Austria and were in widespread use by the 1870s.

Message is written on the other side

POST CARD

THIS CARD MUST BE SENT UNDER COVER ONLY

PLACE STAMP UPON ENVELOPE

THE SPACE BELOW IS FOR THE ADDRESS ONLY.

Address is written here

Sorted post

Operator types post code into keyboard

SORTING AT SPEED
Introduced in the U.S.A. in the 1960s, automatic sorting speeds up the sorting process. The operator punches the post codes into a keyboard, and the letters are sorted by the machine.

Keeping in touch

The invention of the telegraph and the telephone in the 19th century meant that written and verbal messages could be sent quickly over long distances for the first time. Today, people on opposite sides of the globe can talk to each other at the touch of a few buttons.

Magnetic needles

GETTING THE MESSAGE
Early telegraphs could send messages only in coded form. But in 1837, British inventors William Cooke and Charles Wheatstone demonstrated a telegraph that could both send and receive messages letter by letter. Messages were spelled out by magnetic needles, which pointed to individual letters.

Incoming messages are spelled out by magnetic needles.

Outgoing messages are tapped out on buttons.

Wire carrying signal from mouthpiece to receiver

Diaphragm

Mouthpiece

Earpiece

Mouthpiece

TELEPHONE
Alexander Graham Bell invented the telephone in 1876. Telephones like the one shown here, which worked as both the mouthpiece and the receiver, were in use shortly afterwards.

Wire

DIALLING A NUMBER
Before dial telephones were invented, all calls went via an operator. U.S. undertaker Almon Strowger devised the first dial telephone in 1889, after discovering that operators were taking bribes to divert business calls to his competitors.

Numbered dial connects caller via automatic exchange

Coils of wire inside the case carry messages as pulses of electricity.

Liquid crystal display

Numbers are "dialled" on a keypad.

Earpiece

ON THE MOVE
The mobile phone means that telephones need no longer be tied down by wires. The idea originated in the 1940s at the Bell Telephone Laboratories in the U.S.A., but the technology was not available to set up a public service until 30 years later.

In the office

In order to survive and grow, businesses need to be able to communicate quickly and efficiently. Office mechanization began in 1874 with the introduction of the Remington typewriter. Since then, the arrival of photocopiers, fax machines, and other devices has made office tasks much easier.

Reel holding magnetic wire

POULSEN'S TELEGRAPHONE

Carriage return moves paper up to next line

Keys

TAKING MESSAGES
In 1898, Valdemar Poulsen invented the first magnetic voice recorder. It was designed to record conversations so that people couldn't duck out of verbal agreements made over the phone.

TYPEWRITER
Until the invention of the typewriter, all documents were written out by hand. The "QWERTY" keyboard, which has the most often-used letters spaced apart to prevent jamming, was devised by Christopher Scholes in 1873.

QWERTY keyboard

XEROX COPIER
(c.1950)

Early copiers were hand-operated.

Charging chamber

Plate attracts toner

SENDING A FAX

The idea of sending images down a wire was patented by Scotsman Alexander Bain in 1843. Huge facsimile machines were later used by newspapers to send pictures around the world, but it wasn't until the 1980s that fax machines became small enough for office use.

TAKING A COPY

Photocopiers use electrostatic charge to attract black powder (toner) onto the paper. The photocopier was invented in 1938 by American lawyer Chester Carlson, who wanted to copy patent documents quickly and cleanly.

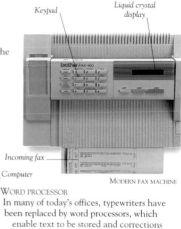

Keypad

Liquid crystal display

Incoming fax

MODERN FAX MACHINE

Screen

Computer

Keyboard

WORD PROCESSOR

In many of today's offices, typewriters have been replaced by word processors, which enable text to be stored and corrections to be made easily. The first word processor, devised by the IBM company in 1964, was the size of a desk and had no screen. Modern word processors are simply personal computers coupled with printers.

Mouse

TRAVEL AND EXPLORATION

INTRODUCTION

THE DESIRE TO TRAVEL by land, sea, or air has inspired many great inventions. From bicycles to biplanes, hundreds of different forms of transport have been devised. The development of sailing ships and navigation led to worldwide exploration, travel, and trade.

GLOBE

FACILE BICYCLE
(1888)

NAVIGATION
Travellers and explorers once depended on maps and globes to navigate long journeys, but advances in electronics have now made travelling safer and easier.

Pedals attached to front wheel

BICYCLES
A relative newcomer in the history of unpowered transport, the bicycle has evolved into one of the most efficient machines ever devised.

Passenger's seat

MOTOR CARS
The first motor car was built in the late 1800s. In just over a century, the car has changed from an expensive and unreliable "horseless carriage" into an everyday form of transport used by millions of people all over the world.

This car had a top speed of 6 km/h (4 mph).

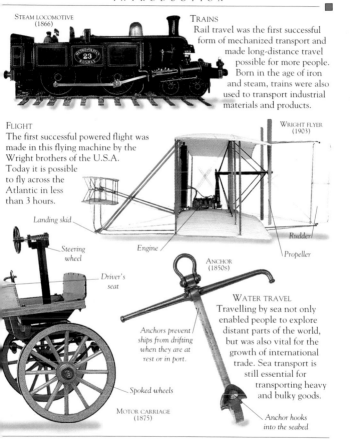

STEAM LOCOMOTIVE
(1866)

TRAINS
Rail travel was the first successful form of mechanized transport and made long-distance travel possible for more people. Born in the age of iron and steam, trains were also used to transport industrial materials and products.

FLIGHT
The first successful powered flight was made in this flying machine by the Wright brothers of the U.S.A. Today it is possible to fly across the Atlantic in less than 3 hours.

WRIGHT FLYER
(1903)

Landing skid

Steering wheel

Engine

Rudder

Propeller

Driver's seat

ANCHOR
(1850s)

WATER TRAVEL
Travelling by sea not only enabled people to explore distant parts of the world, but was also vital for the growth of international trade. Sea transport is still essential for transporting heavy and bulky goods.

Anchors prevent ships from drifting when they are at rest or in port.

Spoked wheels

MOTOR CARRIAGE
(1875)

Anchor hooks into the seabed

WHEELS AND EARLY VEHICLES

DEVISED IN MESOPOTAMIA more than 5,000 years ago, the wheel is one of the most important inventions of all time. As well as being vital for the development of transport, wheels were used by potters for turning clay and also became essential components of later inventions, such as steam engines and clocks.

Cross-piece

Cross-bar

Wooden plank

WHEELS

Early wheels were solid discs cut from tree trunks or assembled from planks of wood. As tools improved, semi-solid and spoked wheels began to appear. These wheels were lighter and made vehicles much easier to handle.

Spokes strengthen the wheel

ROMAN CHARIOT

Lightweight spoked wheel

CHARIOT

The ancient Egyptians used lightweight wheels to make chariots, which were used mainly for warfare. In ancient Rome and Greece, chariots were also used for racing, a popular form of entertainment.

Axle

Roller bearings enable wheel to turn freely

Wheel

Roller bearings

WHEEL BEARINGS
Bearings were invented to reduce the friction between the axle and the wheel so that the wheel turned more easily. Wooden roller bearings like these were probably devised by Danish wagon-makers in about 100 B.C.

WHEEL FACTS

• In some early carts, the axle was fixed to the wheels and rotated as the wheels turned.

• Carriage wheels had to be oiled daily until the invention of the self-oiling axle in 1787.

• Before springs were added, carriages were suspended from straps.

CARRIAGE SPRING

Metal bands hold layers of steel together

HORSE-DRAWN CARRIAGE

Layers (or "leaves") of steel

A SMOOTHER RIDE
Elliptical (or oval-shaped) springs were devised by Obadiah Elliot in 1805 and used on horse-drawn carriages to give a smoother ride.

When the carriage hit a bump, the leaves of steel would bend and then spring back into shape.

Spring attached to the body of the carriage

HORSE POWER

HORSES WERE USED as pack animals as long ago as 4500 B.C. and were first ridden about 2,000 years later. Saddles and bridles made horses easier to ride and control, but it wasn't until the invention of the padded collar that horses could be used to pull carriages, carts, and other heavy loads.

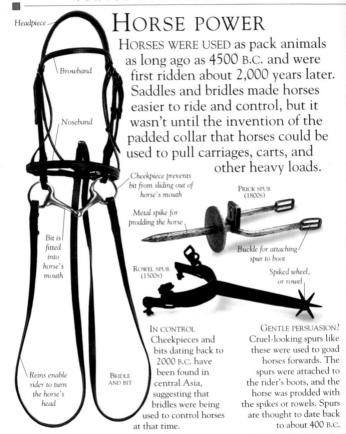

Headpiece

Browband

Noseband

Cheekpiece prevents bit from sliding out of horse's mouth

Bit is fitted into horse's mouth

Reins enable rider to turn the horse's head

BRIDLE AND BIT

PRICK SPUR (1800s)

Metal spike for prodding the horse

Buckle for attaching spur to boot

ROWEL SPUR (1500s)

Spiked wheel, or rowel

IN CONTROL
Cheekpieces and bits dating back to 2000 B.C. have been found in central Asia, suggesting that bridles were being used to control horses at that time.

GENTLE PERSUASION? Cruel-looking spurs like these were used to goad horses forwards. The spurs were attached to the rider's boots, and the horse was prodded with the spikes or rowels. Spurs are thought to date back to about 400 B.C.

HIPPOSANDAL

FOOTWEAR
The Romans used iron "hipposandals" to protect their horses' feet on rough or stony ground. Hoof-shaped shoes, which appeared in Europe in about A.D. 800 and are still used today, are more practical for travelling quickly.

Horse's hoof fits on flat surface

Loop for attaching strap

Ornate fretwork

SADDLE
The invention of the saddle led to a safer and more comfortable journey, both for the rider and the horse. The first saddles, little more than rugs, were used in Siberia from about 600 B.C.

Seat

Pommel

TIBETAN SADDLE
(18TH CENTURY)

CHINESE STIRRUP
(1800s)

Stirrup hangs from the saddle

Rider's foot is placed here

STIRRUPS
Stirrups were invented in Asia and spread to China in the 5th century. They had a big impact on warfare because they helped horsemen to balance more easily as they brandished their weapons.

PULLING A LOAD
Early attempts to get horses to pull heavy loads failed because the harnesses used caused the horses to choke. The rigid padded collar, which fits round the horse's neck, was invented so that horses could pull heavy loads while breathing normally.

WATER TRAVEL

FOR CENTURIES, PEOPLE have tried to find new ways to travel on water. After discovering how to harness the wind, early explorers and travellers took to the seas in simple sail boats. The invention of the steam engine and the arrival of new ship-building materials led to bigger and faster vessels that dominated long-distance travel until the jet age.

STEERING STRAIGHT
Early ships were steered with an oar placed over the side of the vessel. The more effective stern-post rudder, which was attached to the back of the boat, appeared in Europe in about 1200.

Rudder blade

STERN-POST RUDDER

SAILS AND RIGGING
The first sailing boats had square sails and always travelled in the direction of the wind. Triangular lateen sails, invented in 200 B.C., enabled boats to sail against the wind.

Lateen sail

LATEEN SAIL BOAT

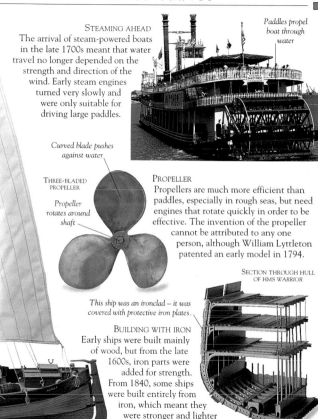

STEAMING AHEAD
The arrival of steam-powered boats in the late 1700s meant that water travel no longer depended on the strength and direction of the wind. Early steam engines turned very slowly and were only suitable for driving large paddles.

Paddles propel boat through water

Curved blade pushes against water

THREE-BLADED PROPELLER

Propeller rotates around shaft

PROPELLER
Propellers are much more efficient than paddles, especially in rough seas, but need engines that rotate quickly in order to be effective. The invention of the propeller cannot be attributed to any one person, although William Lyttleton patented an early model in 1794.

SECTION THROUGH HULL OF HMS WARRIOR

This ship was an ironclad – it was covered with protective iron plates.

BUILDING WITH IRON
Early ships were built mainly of wood, but from the late 1600s, iron parts were added for strength. From 1840, some ships were built entirely from iron, which meant they were stronger and lighter and could carry heavier loads.

RAIL TRAVEL

LONG BEFORE THE FIRST locomotives were built, wagons carrying heavy loads were hauled along tracks by humans or horses. But with the invention of the steam engine came the first self-propelled trains, which were to revolutionize travel all over the world.

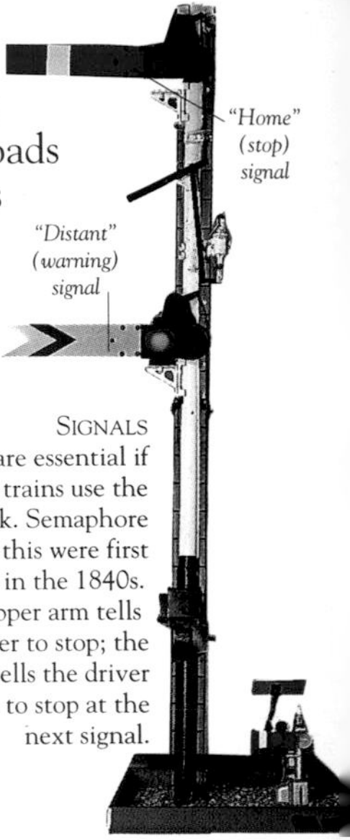

"Home" (stop) signal

"Distant" (warning) signal

SIGNALS
Signals are essential if two or more trains use the same track. Semaphore signals like this were first used in the 1840s. The upper arm tells the driver to stop; the lower arm tells the driver to prepare to stop at the next signal.

MECHANICAL SEMAPHORE SIGNAL

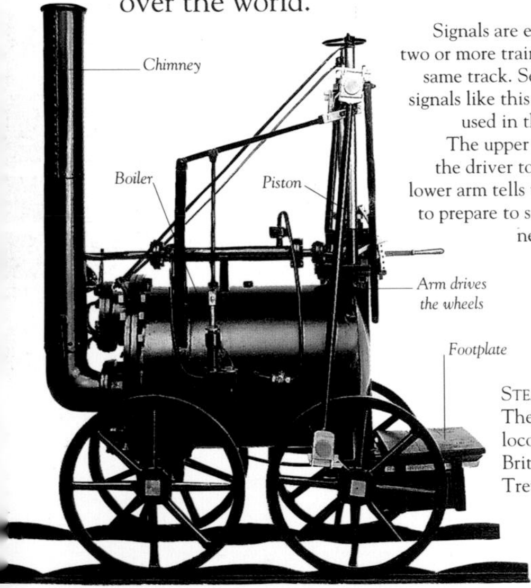

Chimney

Boiler

Piston

Arm drives the wheels

Footplate

STEAM LOCOMOTIVE
The world's first steam locomotive, built by British inventor Richard Trevithick, ran in 1804. The engine pulled a train carrying 70 people over a distance of 16 km (10 miles).

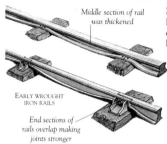

Middle section of rail was thickened

EARLY WROUGHT IRON RAILS

End sections of rails overlap making joints stronger

MAKING TRACKS
Early rails were made of cast iron and often broke under the strain of heavy locomotives. Gradually, these rails were replaced by stronger wrought iron tracks. Steel rails, which are stronger still, appeared in 1857.

DIESEL POWER
Invented in 1892, the diesel engine generates electricity, which can be used to turn the wheels of a train. The first diesel-electric locomotive ran in 1923.

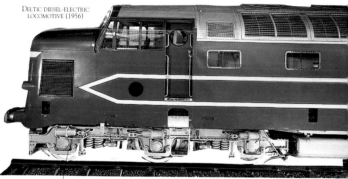

DELTIC DIESEL-ELECTRIC LOCOMOTIVE (1956)

Wheels driven by electric motors

MAGLEV TRAINS
During the 1950s, British engineer Eric Laithwaite developed a motor that could suspend a train above the tracks by magnetic levitation. Although currently used on only a small scale, these Maglev trains may become the trains of the future.

PEDAL POWER

CYCLING IS ONE of the simplest and cheapest ways to travel. Invented about 200 years ago, the first bicycles required great skill and courage to ride. But the addition of steering, pedals, and brakes made cycling a less dangerous form of transport.

A BICYCLE MADE FOR TWO

BEFORE PEDALS
The hobby horse was the forerunner of the bicycle. It consisted of a wooden beam set above two spoked wheels. The rider would sit astride the machine and push the ground with alternate feet. German Baron Karl von Drais produced a machine with steering in 1818.

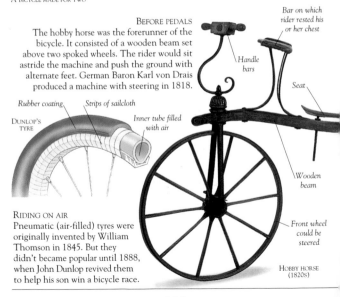

Bar on which rider rested his or her chest

Handle bars

Seat

Rubber coating   *Strips of sailcloth*

DUNLOP'S TYRE

Inner tube filled with air

Wooden beam

Front wheel could be steered

HOBBY HORSE (1820s)

RIDING ON AIR
Pneumatic (air-filled) tyres were originally invented by William Thomson in 1845. But they didn't became popular until 1888, when John Dunlop revived them to help his son win a bicycle race.

CHANGING GEAR
Cycling uphill became much easier after the addition of derailleur gears in 1896. Gears enable the wheels to turn at different speeds while the cyclist pedals normally.

Pedal

DERAILLEUR GEARS

Large cog turns wheels slowly

Small cog turns wheels quickly

Chain

SAFETY FIRST
The penny farthing bicycle, with its huge front wheel, was popular in the 1870s but was dangerous to ride. In 1885, John Starley devised the safety bicycle, which had equal-sized wheels with the saddle in between.

STARLEY'S SAFETY BICYCLE (1885)

Spoked iron wheel

Strong, lightweight steel tubing

Thicker tubing and decorative lugs strengthen the joints.

IMPROVING THE FRAME
In 1898, A. Reynolds patented a way of making steel tubing that was light and strong – ideal for bicycle frames. The tubing was thin for most of its length and thicker at the ends.

109

ON THE ROAD

A FEW STEAM-POWERED carriages ran in the early 1800s, but they were too heavy for road use. It was after the arrival of the internal combustion engine, invented by Etienne Lenoir and improved by Nikolaus Otto, that the first motor cars were built.

STEAM-POWERED
MOTORCYCLE
(1889)

STEAM POWER

Compact steam engines were used in several small road vehicles until about 1910. The first motorcycle, made by the Michaux brothers of France, was in fact steam powered.

THE FIRST CAR

The first car to be sold to the public was made in 1885 by German Karl Benz. The engine was at the back of the car and powered the rear wheels. By 1896, more than 130 cars had been built at the Benz factory.

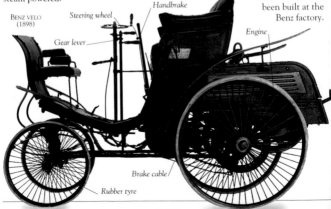

BENZ VELO
(1898)

Handbrake

Steering wheel

Gear lever

Engine

Brake cable

Rubber tyre

CAT'S EYES
One foggy night in 1933, Percy Shaw nearly drove off the edge of the road, but was stopped by the reflection from the eyes of a cat. Shaw went on to invent the cat's-eye roadstud in 1935.

MODERN CAT'S-EYE ROADSTUD

Beads reflect light from car headlamps

RADIAL-PLY TYRES
The arrival of pneumatic tyres in the 1890s made travelling by road more comfortable than on previous solid rubber tyres. In 1949, the Michelin company used radial plies – lengths of wire wound around the tread – to reinforce the rubber. Radial-ply tyres last longer and grip the road better than their predecessors.

Radial plies

TRAFFIC LIGHTS
The first traffic lights, installed in Cleveland, U.S.A. in 1914, had only red and green lights. The amber light was added four years later, and the design is now used all over the world.

Brake disc

Caliper housing pads, which are squeezed against the brake disc

DISC BRAKES
Patented in 1902 by English car-maker Frederick Lanchester, disc brakes are now fitted to all cars. When the brakes are applied, friction pads squeeze the disc and the car slows down.

PIONEERING FLIGHT

SINCE ANCIENT TIMES, the dream of flying has kept many would-be inventors busy. Over the years, brave men and women have tried out an array of flying machines, many of which never left the ground. The first successful flight took place in 1783, when the Montgolfier brothers' hot-air balloon took to the skies.

MONTGOLFIER BALLOON

Passengers' gallery

HOT AIR
Thousands of people watched as the Montgolfier balloon rose into the sky above Paris. The hot air was produced by a straw-burning fire at the mouth of the balloon.

FLYING FACTS

• Helicopters were first proposed by Leonardo da Vinci in the 1400s.

• On its first flight, the Montgolfier balloon carried a duck, a sheep, and a cockerel.

• In 1930, Amy Johnson became the first woman to fly solo from England to Australia.

THE WRIGHT FLYER
In 1903, American bicycle makers Orville and Wilbur Wright built and flew the first powered aeroplane. Their *Flyer* was driven by a lightweight petrol engine and flew a distance of 800 m (half a mile).

Rudder controls direction of plane

Tailplane

Strong wooden frame

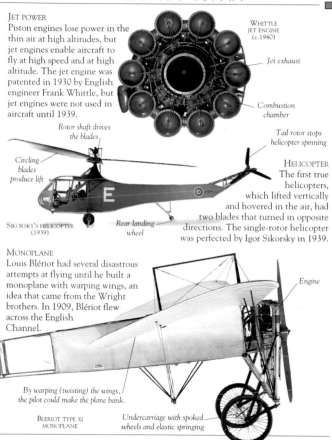

JET POWER
Piston engines lose power in the thin air at high altitudes, but jet engines enable aircraft to fly at high speed and at high altitude. The jet engine was patented in 1930 by English engineer Frank Whittle, but jet engines were not used in aircraft until 1939.

WHITTLE JET ENGINE (c.1940)

Jet exhaust

Combustion chamber

Rotor shaft drives the blades

Circling blades produce lift

Tail rotor stops helicopter spinning

HELICOPTER
The first true helicopters, which lifted vertically and hovered in the air, had two blades that turned in opposite directions. The single-rotor helicopter was perfected by Igor Sikorsky in 1939.

SIKORSKY'S HELICOPTER (1939)

Rear landing wheel

MONOPLANE
Louis Blériot had several disastrous attempts at flying until he built a monoplane with warping wings, an idea that came from the Wright brothers. In 1909, Blériot flew across the English Channel.

Engine

By warping (twisting) the wings, the pilot could make the plane bank.

BLERIOT TYPE XI MONOPLANE

Undercarriage with spoked wheels and elastic springing

THE JET AGE AND SPACE TRAVEL

MODERN TECHNOLOGY has not only made worldwide air travel possible, but has also made the exploration of space a reality. Scientists believe that the aircraft of the future will make use of space technology by travelling in a semi-orbit around the world.

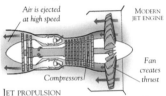

Air is ejected at high speed

MODERN JET ENGINE

Fan creates thrust

Compressors

JET PROPULSION
Jet engines suck in air at the front and eject it at high speed from the back. Spinning blades inside the engine raise the pressure of the air. As the air rushes backwards, the engine is forced forwards.

LIFT-OFF
The Saturn V space rocket was developed in the 1960s in order to send astronauts to the Moon. Because there is no air in space, scientists had to devise special oxygen-rich fuel to power the rocket.

Fuel tanks

SUPERSONIC FLIGHT
Concorde is the only supersonic passenger aircraft. It made its first flight in 1969 and now travels routinely at twice the speed of sound. Concorde can fly from New York to London in less than 3 hours.

SPACE SHUTTLE
Launched by a huge rocket that is later abandoned in space, the Space Shuttle can orbit and then land like an ordinary aircraft. It first flew into space in 1981.

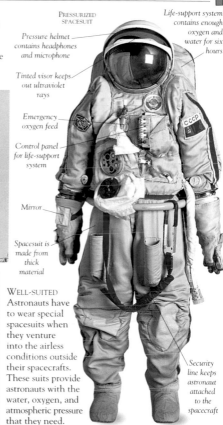

PRESSURIZED SPACESUIT

Pressure helmet contains headphones and microphone

Tinted visor keeps out ultraviolet rays

Emergency oxygen feed

Control panel for life-support system

Mirror

Spacesuit is made from thick material

Life-support system contains enough oxygen and water for six hours

Security line keeps astronaut attached to the spacecraft

SPACE FACTS
• In 1961, Soviet Yuri Gagarin became the first person to travel into space.

• Suits worn by shuttle astronauts weigh 103 kg (227 lb) on Earth, but are weightless in space.

• Saturn V used 13.6 tonnes (tons) of fuel per second on take-off.

WELL-SUITED
Astronauts have to wear special spacesuits when they venture into the airless conditions outside their spacecrafts. These suits provide astronauts with the water, oxygen, and atmospheric pressure that they need.

NAVIGATION

LONG-DISTANCE TRAVEL was unpredictable before navigating instruments were invented. Pioneering explorers had to rely on landmarks, or the position of the stars and planets, in order to work out where they were and to plan their journeys.

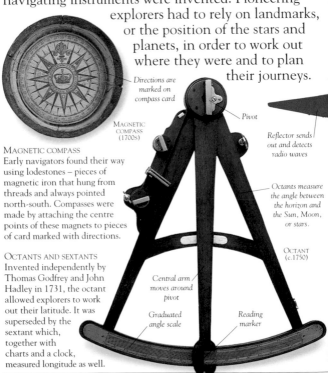

Directions are marked on compass card

MAGNETIC COMPASS (1700s)

Pivot

Reflector sends out and detects radio waves

Octants measure the angle between the horizon and the Sun, Moon, or stars

OCTANT (c.1750)

Central arm moves around pivot

Graduated angle scale

Reading marker

MAGNETIC COMPASS

Early navigators found their way using lodestones – pieces of magnetic iron that hung from threads and always pointed north-south. Compasses were made by attaching the centre points of these magnets to pieces of card marked with directions.

OCTANTS AND SEXTANTS

Invented independently by Thomas Godfrey and John Hadley in 1731, the octant allowed explorers to work out their latitude. It was superseded by the sextant which, together with charts and a clock, measured longitude as well.

MERCATOR PROJECTION MAP
Because they didn't show the effect of the Earth's curved surface, early maps tended to distort distances and directions. In 1569, Gerardus Kremer (known as Mercator) used a special projection technique to draw more accurate maps.

MERCATOR PROJECTION
MAP OF THE WORLD

AIRFIELD RADAR
(1953)

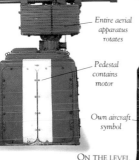

RADAR
Introduced in the late 1930s, radar is vital for both air and water travel. By reflecting radio waves from solid objects, radar enables pilots to "see" obstacles at night or in misty conditions.

Entire aerial apparatus rotates

Pedestal contains motor

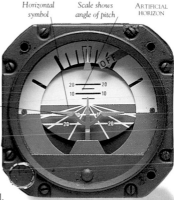

Horizontal symbol

Scale shows angle of pitch

ARTIFICIAL HORIZON

Own aircraft symbol

ON THE LEVEL
Flying aircraft through cloud can confuse even the most experienced pilots. In 1929, Elmer Sperry devised the artificial horizon, which shows the pilot whether the plane is level.

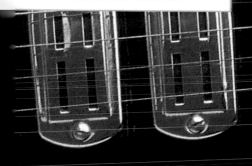

ENTERTAINMENT AND LEISURE

INTRODUCTION

OVER THE CENTURIES, various forms of entertainment and leisure have evolved. Until a hundred years ago, people made their own entertainment, or went out to hear music or see a play. But advances in science and technology have allowed the development of various new kinds of entertainment, many of which can be brought into people's homes.

ENJOYING MUSIC
For thousands of years, people have enjoyed both making and listening to music. This pastime has led to a huge variety of musical instruments and an equally vast range of musical styles.

PORTUGUESE LUTE (1880s)

CYLINDER RECORDER (c.1905)

Horn

Sounds stored on drum

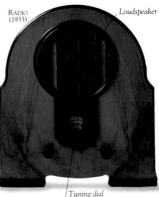

RADIO (1933)

Loudspeaker

Tuning dial

RECORDING
Listening to recorded sounds became possible in 1877, when Thomas Edison devised a way of storing sounds onto a rotating cylinder.

RADIO
Around 1915, a number of inventions made it possible to transmit speech and music. By the early 1920s, eager "wireless" listeners were tuning in to the first regular radio broadcasts.

TELEVISION

In 1936, when television was first broadcast regularly, critics thought that it wouldn't interest people for very long. But within less than half a century, television had become one of the most popular sources of entertainment.

CINEMA

The invention of the magic lantern and other image projectors led to the growth of the cinema. After the arrival of "talkies" (films with soundtracks) in 1927, the industry boomed.

MAGIC
LANTERN
(1908)

Projection lens

Slide holder

Counters

Viewing window for acetylene lamp or candle

BACKGAMMON SET
(EARLY 1800s)

PLAYING GAMES

Much ingenuity has gone into the invention of different games and toys. Many games, such as backgammon or chess, can be traced back hundreds or thousands of years. Others, such as electronic and video games, are much more recent inventions.

SOUND AND VISION

MUCH OF OUR ENTERTAINMENT today involves listening to music, going to the cinema, or watching television. Thanks to advances in technology, sounds can now be stored on disc or sent through the airwaves, while moving pictures can cross the globe in an instant.

Fingerholes

SUDANESE WHISTLE

Musical instruments

Music-making is one of the oldest forms of entertainment. Since the first whistles appeared about 40,000 years ago, thousands of different musical instruments have evolved.

Strings

Pickup converts the sound into electrical signals

Hollow soundbox

STRINGS AND BOWS
Bowed fiddles date back to the 10th century. As the bow moves across the strings, the strings vibrate and produce a sound.

Bow

Strings

ELECTRIC GUITAR
In 1932, Adolphus Rickenbacker built the first electric guitar. His instrument was based on a traditional Spanish design.

IRANIAN SPIKE FIDDLE (1700s)

Volume and tone control knobs

RICKENBACKER ELECTRO-ACOUSTIC GUITAR (EARLY 1930S)

PIANO

First built by Bartolomeo Cristofori in 1709, the piano was one of the first keyboard instruments that could play both softly and loudly, depending on how hard the keys were hit.

Fingerboard

Pegs are turned to tune the strings

INSIDE A PIANO

Strings

Hammers strike the strings with varying force

ELECTRONIC KEYBOARD

Display panel

Control panel enables sounds to be varied

ELECTRONIC SOUNDS

Popularized by Robert Moog in the 1970s, electronic synthesizers can produce a wide range of musical sounds at the touch of a few buttons.

Each cymbal is a thin disc made from copper and tin.

Leather strap

CYMBALS

CLASHING CYMBALS

Cymbals have been played since ancient times. These cymbals were made by Zildjian, an old Turkish firm that keeps the exact blend of metals used a closely guarded secret.

Zildjian

MUSIC FACTS

• European musical notation developed in A.D. 800-1100.

• The word *piano* comes from the Italian *piano e forte*, meaning "soft and loud."

• Making a classical guitar takes a lot of wood, about 85% of which is thrown away.

Recording sound

In 1877, Thomas Edison invented the phonograph, a device that could both record and play back sounds. The sounds were stored as indentations on a piece of tinfoil that was wrapped around a rotating drum. Mechanical recording continued until the 1920s, when electric systems first appeared.

Mouthpiece

EDISON'S
PHONOGRAPH

*Horn amplifies
the sound*

*Recording
drum*

THE FIRST RECORDING
Edison's phonograph had a horn (not shown here) attached to the mouthpiece. A needle resting on the drum converted the indentations back into sounds, which were replayed through the horn.

*Needle rests in groove
and vibrates as the
disc revolves*

EARLY
GRAMOPHONE

*Flat disc sits
on turntable*

GRAMOPHONE
The first flat disc record player, or gramophone, was made by Emile Berliner in 1888. The playback mechanism was similar to that of Edison's phonograph, except that the sounds were stored on a flat disc rather than on a cylindrical drum.

TAPE RECORDER
(1950s)

Spools of
magnetic
tape

Loudspeaker

GETTING IT TAPED

Sound was first recorded onto magnetic tape in the 1920s. As the sound is recorded, tiny metal particles on the tape become magnetized. On replay, the particles produce electrical signals, which are reproduced as sound through the loudspeaker.

SONY
WALKMAN

PERSONAL STEREO

The Walkman was invented in 1979 by engineers at the Sony Corporation in Japan. Some thought that the Walkman's inability to record would make it difficult to sell, but it was an instant success.

Cassette
player

Earphones

Sound is stored as
microscopic pits

COMPACT
DISC

COMPACT DISC

Launched in 1982, the compact disc (CD) stores sound digitally as a series of numbers. When it is replayed, the disc is scanned by a laser beam, which reads the encoded sound and allows it to be reproduced clearly.

RECORDING FACTS

• Recorded music first went on sale in 1886.

• Modern magnetic tape came about as a result of scientists trying to improve sticky tape.

• Long-playing vinyl records (LPs) appeared in 1948 and played for five times longer than previous records.

Radio

The invention of the radio transformed the entertainment business and led to a new information age. Radio was developed by Italian scientist Guglielmo Marconi, who started experimenting with radio waves in his parents' attic. In 1894, Marconi succeeded in sending radio waves across a room. By 1901, he was sending radio messages across the Atlantic.

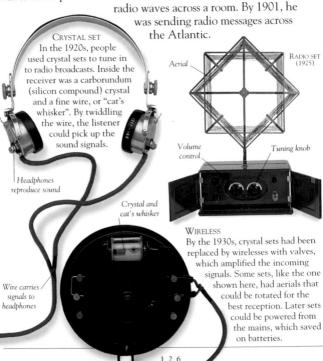

CRYSTAL SET
In the 1920s, people used crystal sets to tune in to radio broadcasts. Inside the receiver was a carborundum (silicon compound) crystal and a fine wire, or "cat's whisker". By twiddling the wire, the listener could pick up the sound signals.

Aerial

RADIO SET
(1925)

Volume control

Tuning knob

Headphones reproduce sound

Crystal and cat's whisker

Wire carries signals to headphones

WIRELESS
By the 1930s, crystal sets had been replaced by wirelesses with valves, which amplified the incoming signals. Some sets, like the one shown here, had aerials that could be rotated for the best reception. Later sets could be powered from the mains, which saved on batteries.

TRANSISTOR RADIO
In the 1950s, radio valves were replaced by transistors, which were smaller and used less power. The first transistor radio was built in 1954.

Tuning dial

Volume control

Microphone cover

RADIO MICROPHONE
The ribbon microphone was used widely for broadcasting from the 1930s until the 1970s. A metallic ribbon inside the cover picked up the sound waves and converted them into electrical signals.

LOUDSPEAKERS
Early loudspeakers had horns, and groups of people would gather round them to listen to the radio. The modern type, which can fill a room with sound, was devised by Kellog and Rice in 1925.

LOUDSPEAKER

Cardboard cone

1960-695

Magnetic field causes cone to vibrate

RIBBON MICROPHONE WITH COVER

Case housing permanent magnet and coil

Photography and film

In 1835, English scientist William Fox Talbot developed a photographic process, the principle of which is still used today. By coating paper with a silver compound, which darkens when exposed to light, he produced a negative image from which positives could be printed. By the 1900s, moving images could be recorded, and the cinema age began.

CAMERA OBSCURA (EARLY 1800S)

Lens

Curtain keeps out the light

CAMERA OBSCURA
The camera obscura had all the makings of a camera, but couldn't record images. As light shone through a small hole or a lens, an image was projected onto a flat surface inside the box.

Plate holder

BOXES OF ROLL-FILM

Roll-film was essential for later movie cameras

ROLL-FILM
In 1885, George Eastman devised rolls of plastic film to replace bulky photographic plates. Eastman also introduced a roll-film camera, which was both cheap and easy to use.

Rear section slides in and out to alter size of image

Plate coated with light-sensitive chemicals

PLATE CAMERA
Photographic cameras that recorded images on plates, or glass sheets, were introduced in 1851. The plate was exposed for up to 30 seconds to capture a negative image.

Lens tube

Fine-focusing control

Lens cover

PLATE CAMERA (1850S)

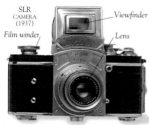

SLR CAMERA (1937)
Film winder — Viewfinder — Lens

A CLEARER PICTURE
A single-lens reflex (SLR) camera allows the photographer to see the exact image that will be recorded. A mirror and a prism inside the camera reflect the light from the lens to the viewfinder.

ON THE MOVE
Moving pictures are created by taking a series of still images in quick succession. The first successful movie camera was made in 1895 by the Lumière brothers of France.

Film passes from top to bottom compartment

Lens

Bottom compartment

MOVIE CAMERA (1909)

FILMING IN COLOUR
This Technicolor camera recorded incoming light on separate films that were sensitive to red, blue, and green light. The films were then combined to make a full-colour print that was projected onto a screen.

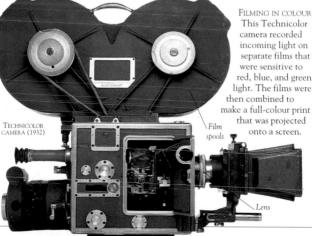

TECHNICOLOR CAMERA (1932)

Film spools

Lens

Television and video

John Logie Baird first demonstrated television in 1926 at the Selfridge's store in London, and by 1934 more than 10,000 of his "televisors" had been sold. But the arrival of all-electronic television, which used cathode ray tubes, soon made the televisor obsolete and led to the first high-definition television broadcast.

Speed control

Synchronizing control

TELEVISOR (1926)

Screen

TELEVISOR
Baird's televisor worked on a system of spinning discs, which had been devised in 1884 by German scientist Paul Nipkow. The discs scanned the moving image and converted it into a series of electrical impulses, producing a poor-quality image on a tiny screen.

ELECTRONIC TELEVISION
By the late 1930s, all televisions used cathode ray tubes. The tubes projected electrons onto the screen, producing images of much higher quality than Baird's mechanical device could ever have done.

Tuning control

Volume control

TELEVISION (1950s)

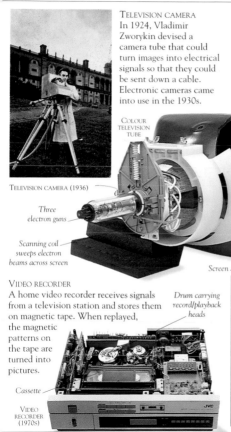

TELEVISION CAMERA
In 1924, Vladimir Zworykin devised a camera tube that could turn images into electrical signals so that they could be sent down a cable. Electronic cameras came into use in the 1930s.

TELEVISION CAMERA (1936)

WATCHING IN COLOUR
Inside a colour television, three cathode ray tubes are combined into one. Each one shows pictures in either red, green, or blue, and the mixture of these colours on screen gives a full-colour picture.

COLOUR TELEVISION TUBE

Three electron guns

Scanning coil sweeps electron beams across screen

Screen

VIDEO RECORDER
A home video recorder receives signals from a television station and stores them on magnetic tape. When replayed, the magnetic patterns on the tape are turned into pictures.

Drum carrying record/playback heads

Cassette

VIDEO RECORDER (1970s)

JVC

TELEVISION FACTS

• In 1936, a television set cost nearly as much as a small car.

• Colour television was first broadcast successfully in 1953.

• Built in 1956, the first video recorder was the size of a piano and recorded onto tape that was 5 cm (2 in) wide.

GAMES AND TOYS

PEOPLE HAVE ALWAYS entertained themselves with games or toys of some kind. Some of the games played today can be traced back to ancient times, while others are more recent inventions. Many games look incredibly simple, but the basic rules are often the product of an inventive mind.

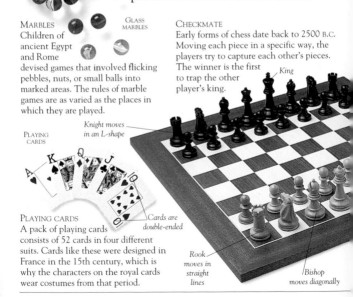

MARBLES

GLASS MARBLES

Children of ancient Egypt and Rome devised games that involved flicking pebbles, nuts, or small balls into marked areas. The rules of marble games are as varied as the places in which they are played.

PLAYING CARDS

Knight moves in an L-shape

PLAYING CARDS
A pack of playing cards consists of 52 cards in four different suits. Cards like these were designed in France in the 15th century, which is why the characters on the royal cards wear costumes from that period.

Cards are double-ended

CHECKMATE
Early forms of chess date back to 2500 B.C. Moving each piece in a specific way, the players try to capture each other's pieces. The winner is the first to trap the other player's king.

King

Rook moves in straight lines

Bishop moves diagonally

GAME AND TOY FACTS

- The first patented toy was a mechanical horse designed to teach people how to ride.
- Modern playing cards are based on Tarot cards, which were used for fortune-telling.
- Chess is derived from *chaturanga*, a Hindu dice game.

DOMINOES

The game of dominoes originated in China and spread to Europe via Italian silk and spice traders. It is now played throughout the world.

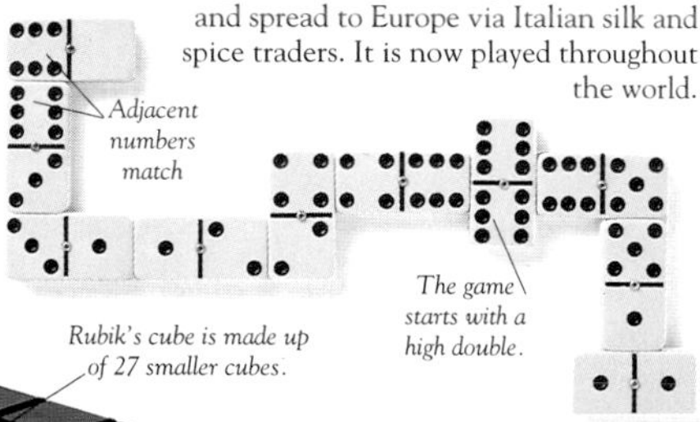

Adjacent numbers match

The game starts with a high double.

Rubik's cube is made up of 27 smaller cubes.

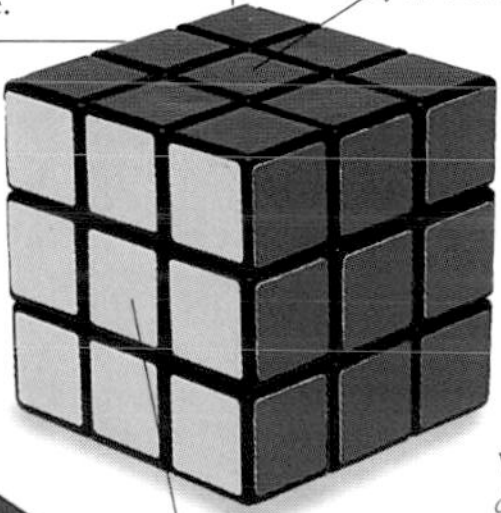

RUBIK'S CUBE

Each face of the cube can pivot around the centre.

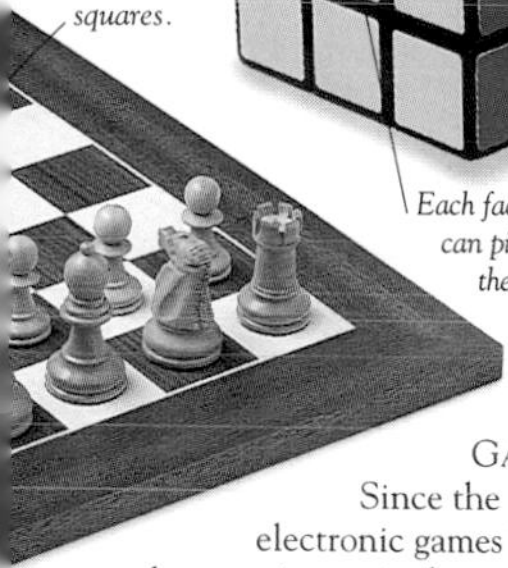

A chessboard has 32 dark squares and 32 light squares.

RUBIK'S CUBE

In 1980, Hungarian professor Ernö Rubik introduced a simple but infuriating puzzle that was to make him a multi-millionaire. The object of the puzzle is to arrange the cube as it is shown here, so that each face is a uniform colour.

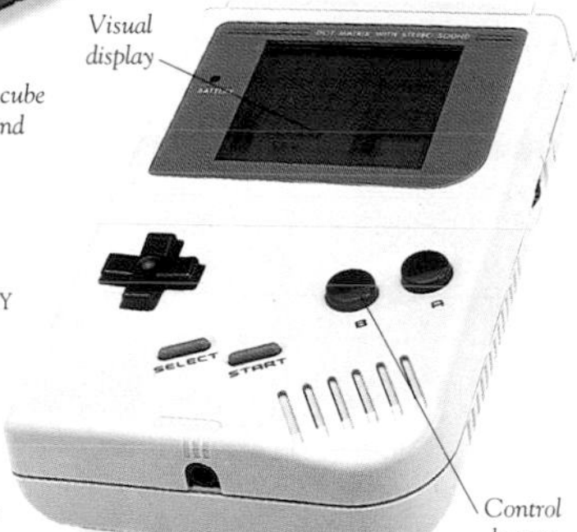

GAME BOY

Visual display

Control button

GAME BOY

Since the 1970s, electronic games have become increasingly popular. In 1989, the Nintendo company of Japan launched the Game Boy, a hand-held video game player that proved popular with children of all ages.

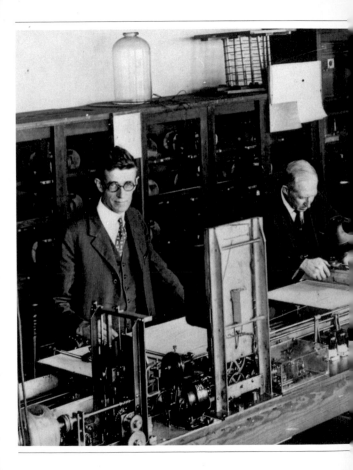

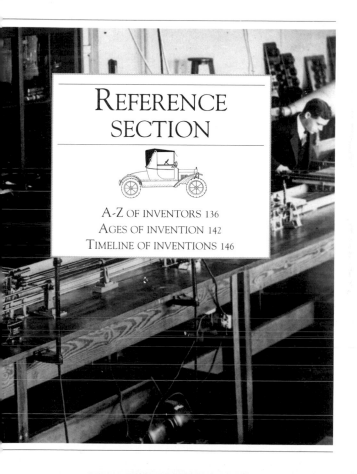

REFERENCE
SECTION

A-Z OF INVENTORS

THE STORY OF INVENTION is one of human ingenuity and imagination. Many of the people who were inspired to invent objects that changed our world are as fascinating to read about as their creations. Here is a selection of some of the most interesting inventors.

ARCHIMEDES

Greek mathematician and inventor Archimedes (c.287-212 B.C.) is famous for leaping from his bath with a loud cry of "Eureka!", because he had worked out how and why things floated. He invented the siege engine, which the ancient Greeks used in battle, and gave his name to a screw pump used for raising water. He also founded the science of hydrostatics – the study of the forces exerted by fluids.

ARCHIMEDES' SCREW

BELL, ALEXANDER GRAHAM

Alexander Graham Bell (1847-1922) was born in Scotland and emigrated to Canada in 1870. A teacher of the deaf, Bell was interested in trying to convert speech into electrical signals that could be sent down a wire. He patented the first working telephone in 1876, and a year later he travelled to England to promote his invention. Bell joined forces with American inventor Thomas Edison, and together they built several new telephones.

DA VINCI, LEONARDO

Italian artist Leonardo da Vinci (1452-1519) produced drawings of many complex machines, some of which suggested ways of travelling at speed, or even flying. Unfortunately, it was not possible to construct any of these machines in an age when there were neither the materials nor the technical know-how to build them.

RECONSTRUCTION OF ONE OF DA VINCI'S FLYING MACHINES

DAIMLER, GOTTLIEB

DAIMLER'S MOTORCYCLE (1882)

Gottlieb Daimler (1834-1900) built the first roadworthy motor vehicle in 1885. In 1926, he joined forces with fellow German Karl Benz, and together they formed the successful Daimler-Benz motor company. Daimler also worked closely with engineer Nikolaus Otto to develop a lightweight, high-speed engine that could run on petrol. He first tried out his engine on a strange wooden-framed motorcycle (shown here).

EDISON, THOMAS

American Thomas Edison (1847-1931) was expelled from school because his teachers thought he was a slow learner. Despite this, he became one of the world's greatest inventors. In 1871, Edison devised a ticker-tape machine, which brought financial news instantly to stock exchanges. The profits from this invention enabled him to set up a research laboratory and turn invention into an industry. His later inventions included the electric light bulb and the gramophone.

FARADAY, MICHAEL

ROTATION APPARATUS (1821)

The son of a blacksmith, British scientist Michael Faraday (1791-1867) was apprenticed to a bookbinder. The books that he worked with sparked off a keen interest in science, and in 1813 he started work as an assistant at London's Royal Institution. Although he was not strictly an inventor, Faraday discovered various electrical principles that were used in other inventions, such as the telephone, the electric motor, and the transformer.

GALILEI, GALILEO

At a time when European scientists still clung to ancient Greek ideas, Italian Galileo Galilei (1564-1642) challenged many people's beliefs. Galileo was a mathematician, an astronomer, and a philosopher who came up with many ingenious inventions, from a primitive thermometer to an improved telescope. He also discovered that the swing of a pendulum could be used to regulate a clock, and that the Earth moves around the Sun.

GUTENBERG, JOHANNES
German-born Johannes Gutenberg (1400-1468) is regarded as the inventor of printing. Although the Chinese had invented ways of printing hundreds of years earlier, Gutenberg brought several techniques together, making the printing process much less laborious. His most ingenious invention was the idea of casting individual letters that could be assembled quickly into a block of type and fitted into a printing press.

HOOKE, ROBERT
Robert Hooke (1635-1703) was a British scientist and architect who was asked to oversee the rebuilding of London after the Great Fire in 1666. During his lifetime, Hooke came up with several important inventions, including a balance spring for regulating watches, various instruments for navigation, and an improved microscope that enabled him to carry out important biological studies.

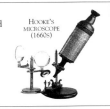

HOOKE'S MICROSCOPE (1660S)

HUYGENS, CHRISTIAAN
The son of a Dutch poet, Christiaan Huygens (1629-1693) developed Galileo's ideas of the effect of gravity and the motions of the planets. He was interested in lenses and telescopes and suggested that light travels in waves. He was the first to see Saturn's rings, and he also discovered Saturn's fourth moon. Huygens used Galileo's discovery of the regular swing of a pendulum to build the first pendulum clock.

KAY, JOHN
John Kay (1704-c.1780) was born in England and educated in France. He invented the flying shuttle, which was eagerly adopted by textile manufacturers who wanted to increase their output, but who refused to give Kay any money for his idea. In 1753, Kay's house was attacked by angry textile workers who had lost their jobs as a result of his invention. Kay fled to France, where he died in poverty.

HAND LOOM

KNIGHT, MARGARET

American inventor Margaret Knight (1839-1914) designed a machine for making the square-based paper bags that are popular in the U.S.A. for carrying groceries. Knight's invention brought her a great deal of public attention, as social convention in the 19th century meant that there were very few female inventors. Her local newspaper described her as a "woman Edison".

KNIGHT'S PAPER BAG MACHINE (1879)

LIPPERSHEY, HANS

Dutch spectacle-maker Hans Lippershey (c.1570-1619) realized that lenses could do more than just correct his clients' eyesight. He used convex (outward-curving) lenses to correct long sight and concave (inward-curving) lenses to correct short sight. When he looked through both lenses together, Lippershey found that distant objects appeared closer. This discovery led to the invention of the telescope, which he patented in 1608.

LISTER, JOSEPH

British surgeon Joseph Lister (1827-1912) was greatly influenced by his father (also called Joseph), who designed a fine microscope that he used to examine blood cells and body tissues. Continuing the family tradition, Lister made important discoveries about blood clotting and the inflammation of blood vessels. He also introduced antiseptics, which dramatically reduced the incidents of death during surgery.

ANTISEPTIC SPRAY (1875)

MAIMAN, THEODORE

American physicist Theodore Maiman (b.1927) gained a PhD in 1955 and started work on a maser, a device that was used to detect radio waves from space. Maiman came up with the idea of using the same principle to produce light, and in 1960 he built the first working laser. The laser light was more intense than anything that had been seen before, and it now has all kinds of uses from bar code readers to delicate surgery.

MARCONI, MARCHESE GUGLIELMO

Guglielmo Marconi (1874-1937) had an Irish mother and an Italian father. In 1894 he began experimenting with radio waves, which had been discovered six years earlier by German scientist Heinrich Hertz. Marconi invented an aerial that increased the range of transmission and soon realized that "wireless" messages could reach almost anywhere. In 1901, he sent the first radio message from Europe across the Atlantic.

RADIO AERIAL

MONTGOLFIER, JOSEPH AND JACQUES

French brothers Joseph (1740-1810) and Jacques (1745-1799) Montgolfier were the sons of a paper-bag manufacturer. After noticing that paper bags filled with hot air could float upwards, they set about building the world's first hot-air balloon. Made from reinforced flameproof paper, and filled with hot air from a fire below, the balloon made its first successful flight in 1783.

MORSE, SAMUEL

American portrait painter Samuel Morse (1791-1872) was interested in using electricity and magnetism to send messages over long distances. Working at the same time as telegraph inventors Charles Wheatstone and William Cooke, Morse devised his famous dot-dash code, which is still used today. The code saves time because the most common letters have the shortest codes.

MORSE CODE MACHINE

SHOCKLEY, WILLIAM

Together with John Bardeen and William Brattain, William Shockley (1910-1989) made the first working transistor on Christmas Eve, 1947. For years, Shockley's team had searched for a replacement for valves, which were used in early televisions, radios, and computers. Valves were bulky and unreliable, and gave off a lot of heat. Transistors began to replace valves by 1960, and led directly to the complex yet tiny "chips", which are universal in modern electronics.

WATT, JAMES

James Watt (1736-1819) was a Scotsman who made scientific instruments for a living. In 1763, after studying the pumping

action of Newcomen's steam engine, Watt made some improvements that enabled the engine to drive wheels, paddles, and propellers. These improvements, which involved turning the up-and-down motion of the piston into rotation, had a huge impact on Europe's Industrial Revolution.

WHITTLE, FRANK

Frank Whittle (b.1907) joined the Royal Air Force in 1923 and patented the jet engine seven years later. The engine was built for high-speed, high-altitude flight, and was to replace the piston engine, which could not work in the cold, thin air at high altitudes. However, the first jet engines were not built until the late 1930s, when the metals needed to withstand the high temperatures in the new engine became available.

WHITTLE'S JET ENGINE (c.1940)

WRIGHT, ORVILLE AND WILBUR

American brothers Orville (1871-1948) and Wilbur (1867-1912) Wright were self-taught aeronauts. In 1903, they built

and flew the world's first successful powered aeroplane. Because they were bicycle-makers by trade, the brothers knew how to make machines both light and strong. By 1905, their *Flyer III* could turn and bank, fly in circles, and perform figures-of-eight.

ZWORYKIN, VLADIMIR

Vladimir Zworykin (1889-1982) studied physics in Leningrad and emigrated to the U.S.A. in 1919. Zworykin was obsessed with television, and in 1923 he devised the iconoscope, an essential component of the electronic television camera. Six years later, he went to work for the Radio Corporation of America, who believed that television would become big business. Despite America's head start, Britain's television service was the first on the air in 1936.

AGES OF INVENTION

WHEN AND WHERE did inventions originate? From ancient times until recent years, many inventions can be linked to specific times and places. The ancient civilizations of Mesopotamia,

WHEEL

Egypt, Greece, and Rome were all important centres of invention, while more recent innovations from Europe, North America, and the Pacific Rim have been important for economic and industrial growth.

Invention in the ancient world

By about 500 B.C., many fundamental inventions and discoveries had already been made. Metalworking, building, surveying, and measuring were all developed in their basic forms by the end of the first millenium B.C. This period also saw the birth of science, as philosophers craved a greater knowledge and understanding of how things worked.

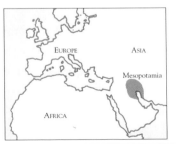

EUROPE

ASIA

Mesopotamia

AFRICA

EARLY POTTERS

MESOPOTAMIA
About 5,500 years ago, at the start of the Bronze Age, several cities were emerging in the region between the Euphrates and Tigris rivers – an area later known as Mesopotamia. The people who lived in this "cradle of civilization" came up with many great inventions, including the wheel, which was used for pottery and transport.

ANCIENT EGYPT
Egypt was reaching the peak of its power and achievement by

PYRAMID

about 1500 B.C. Around this time, the Egyptians devised ways of moving huge stones, which enabled them to construct pyramids, temples, and other impressive structures. They were also pioneers in boat-building, sailing, and the use of early medical treatments.

ANCIENT GREECE
From around the 6th century B.C., the Mediterranean region was ruled by

THE PARTHENON

the Greeks. The Greeks were accomplished architects and keen travellers, navigators, and seafarers. Greek philosophers introduced new ways of thinking, which influenced technology and laid the foundations of modern science.

ANCIENT ROME
By A.D. 100, the Roman Empire had spread from northern Europe to

ROAD-BUILDING

north Africa and the eastern Mediterranean. Such conquests demanded invention for war machines, transport, and communication. The invention of concrete enabled the Romans to build a huge network of roads, some of which are still used today.

Invention in the modern world

Many inventions that are used today had their origins in China. Some of these inventions remained unknown to the rest of the world for many years, but a few were taken to Europe by travelling merchants and re-emerged there in around the 14th century. At the close of the 20th century, Japan, Taiwan, and other countries of the Pacific Rim have become important centres of invention and innovation, and are now enjoying the world's fastest economic growth.

PRINTING

CHINA

From about 1000 B.C. to about A.D. 1000, a stream of ideas and inventions were emerging in China. In particular, the rule of the T'ang emperors (A.D. 618-906) was a time of great innovation. Among other things, the Chinese invented paper, printing, gunpowder, the magnetic compass, and a fine porcelain, which is still called "china".

NAVIGATING INSTRUMENTS

RENAISSANCE

In the 14th and 15th centuries, a renaissance (or rebirth) of interest in Greek and Roman art, architecture, and literature swept across Europe. This period also saw the growth of modern science and the arrival of many new inventions, which were brought to Europe by Greek scholars fleeing from their Turkish enemies.

INDUSTRIAL REVOLUTION
The Industrial Revolution began in England and spread rapidly through Europe during the 18th century. It was a period of great innovation, triggered off by the use of water and then steam power to extract natural resources and to provide the energy and power needed for industry and transport.

STEAM LOCOMOTIVE

UNITED STATES OF AMERICA
In the 19th century, the U.S.A. emerged as a powerful industrial nation. A rapidly growing population and a continent with unlimited natural resources provided the key to this growth. During this time, the U.S.A. made advances in many areas of industry, including communication, transport, engineering, and entertainment.

SKYSCRAPER

BULLET TRAIN

PACIFIC RIM
For centuries, differences in religion and culture kept the East and the West divided. Japan was the first country to rise above this, and by the 1970s Japanese companies were producing cars, motorcycles, and electronic goods that sold all over the world. Today, the success of industry in the Pacific Rim is overtaking that of the West.

TIMELINE OF INVENTIONS

EXAMPLES OF HUMAN INVENTION and discovery can be traced back hundreds of thousands of years. The charts on the following pages list some key inventions and show how invention has progressed from early times to the present day.

20,000 B.C.			A.D. 1
	15,000 B.C.	10,000 B.C.	5000 B.C.

INVENTIONS

• BONE NEEDLES (c.20,000 B.C.) • PAINTBRUSH (c.18,000 B.C.) • MAMMOTH-BONE HUTS (c.18,000 B.C.)	• HARPOONS (c.13,000 B.C.) • BASKET-WEAVING (c.12,000 B.C.) • POTTERY VESSELS (c.10,500 B.C.)	• FISHING NETS (c.10,000 B.C.) • GRINDSTONES (c.10,000 B.C.) • COMB (c.8000 B.C.) • DUGOUT BOATS (c.7500 B.C.) • SPINDLE (c.7000 B.C.) • COPPER-SMELTING (c.6500 B.C.) • BRICKS (c.6000 B.C.) • WHEELS (c.5500 B.C.)	• SAILING VESSELS (4000-3500 B.C.) • PLOUGH (c.3500 B.C.) • CUNEIFORM SCRIPT (c.3300 B.C.) • ABACUS (c.3000 B.C.) • BARBED FISH HOOKS (c.3000 B.C.) • HORSERIDING (c.2000 B.C.) • CALENDAR (1747 B.C.) • IRON-SMELTING (c.1500 B.C.) • COINS (c.600 B.C.)

WORLD EVENTS

• c.20,000 B.C. Stone tools are developed. • c.18,000 B.C. The last ice age reaches its coldest phase.	• c.13,000 B.C. The last ice age ends. • c.11,000 B.C. Dogs are domesticated.	• c.10,000 B.C. Woolly mammoths become extinct. • c.8000 B.C. Crop farming begins in the Middle East.	• c.3500 B.C. The Bronze Age begins. • c.2400 B.C. The first city-states are established in Mesopotamia.

	A.D. 1		A.D. 1500
		A.D. 500	A.D. 1000
EVERYDAY LIFE	• DOMED ROOF (c.A.D. 124)		• SPECTACLES (A.D. 1268) • MECHANICAL CLOCK (A.D. 1280)
TRADE AND INDUSTRY	• HORSESHOES (c.A.D. 50) • WHEELBARROW (A.D. 200-300)	• WINDMILL (A.D. 650) • PAPER MONEY (A.D. 800-900) • WHEELED PLOUGH (A.D. 950)	• STANDARD YARD (A.D. 1305) • OIL PAINTS (A.D. 1400)
SCIENCE AND COMMUNICATION	• PAPER (A.D. 105)	• BOOK-PRINTING (A.D. 868) • GUNPOWDER (A.D. 800-900)	• LENSES (c.A.D. 1000) • CAMERA OBSCURA (c.A.D. 1000) • PRINTING PRESS (A.D. 1450)
TRAVEL AND EXPLORATION	• STIRRUPS (A.D. 350) • ASTROLABE (A.D. 400-500)		• PADDED HORSE COLLAR (A.D. 900-1000) • MAGNETIC COMPASS (A.D. 1100) • STERN-POST RUDDER (c.A.D. 1200)
ENTERTAINMENT AND LEISURE			• MUSICAL NOTATION (A.D. 800-1100)
WORLD EVENTS	• A.D. 100 The Romans set up trade links with southern India and Sri Lanka. • A.D. 300 Christianity becomes the official religion of the Roman Empire.	• A.D. 600 Islam spreads through the Middle East and northern Africa. • A.D. 618 The T'ang dynasty rises to power in China.	• A.D. 1271 Italian explorer Marco Polo leaves Venice for China. • A.D. 1346 Bubonic plague sweeps through Europe and Asia.

1500			1699
	1550	1600	1650
EVERYDAY LIFE	• WATCH (c.1500)	• FLUSHING TOILET (1596)		• PENDULUM CLOCK (1657) • SPIRIT LEVEL (1661)
TRADE AND INDUSTRY	• LACE-MAKING (1500s)	• STOCKING FRAME (1589)		
SCIENCE AND COMMUNICATION		• PENCIL (1565) • COMPOUND MICROSCOPE (1590)	• REFRACTING TELESCOPE (1608) • PASCAL'S CALCULATOR (1642)	• IMPROVED MICROSCOPE (1665) • REFLECTING TELESCOPE (1668)
TRAVEL AND EXPLORATION		• MERCATOR PROJECTION MAP (1569)	• STAGE COACH (c.1620) • SUBMARINE (1620)	
ENTERTAINMENT AND LEISURE				
WORLD EVENTS	• 1526 The powerful Moghul empire is founded in India. • c.1530 The trans-Atlantic slave trade is established.	• 1520 The Ottoman empire in Asia reaches its peak. • 1577 Francis Drake sets sail on his round-the-world voyage.	• 1620 Pilgrims land in America aboard the *Mayflower*. • 1644 The Manchu dynasty is founded in China.	• 1680s The Ashanti kingdom of West Africa is established. • 1682 Halley spots the comet that's now named after him.

1700			1899
	1750	1800	1850
EVERYDAY LIFE	• FRANKLIN STOVE (1740)	• OIL LAMP WITH HOLLOW WICK (1784) • VACCINE (1796)	• MATCHES (1827) • LAWN MOWER (1830)	• ELECTRIC LIGHT BULB (c.1880) • COMPACT ELECTRIC MOTOR (1899)
TRADE AND INDUSTRY	• NEWCOMEN'S STEAM ENGINE (1712) • FLYING SHUTTLE (1733)	• WATT'S STEAM ENGINE (1782) • COTTON GIN (1792)	• JACQUARD LOOM (1805) • REAPING MACHINE (1834)	• POWERED WOOL CLIPPERS (1860s) • STEAM TURBINE GENERATOR (1884)
SCIENCE AND COMMUNICATION	• MERCURY THERMOMETER (1714) • CENTIGRADE SCALE (1742)	• LIGHTNING ROD (1752) • SPRING BALANCE (1776) • METRIC SYSTEM (1795)	• BATTERY (1800) • POSTAGE STAMPS (1840) • ANAESTHETICS (1846)	• TYPEWRITER (1870) • TELEPHONE (1876) • RADIO (1894)
TRAVEL AND EXPLORATION	• OCTANT (1731)	• SEXTANT (1757) • HOT-AIR BALLOON (1783) • PROPELLER (1790s)	• STEAM LOCOMOTIVE (1802) • PEDAL BICYCLE (1839) • IRON SHIPS (1840)	• MOTORCAR (1885) • SAFETY BICYCLE (1885) • DIESEL ENGINE (1892)
ENTERTAINMENT AND LEISURE	• PIANO (1709)		• SAXOPHONE (1846)	• PLATE CAMERA (1851) • PHONOGRAPH (1877) • GRAMOPHONE (1888)
WORLD EVENTS	• 1724 The Russian Academy of Sciences is founded. • 1737 Earthquake kills 300,000 people in India.	• 1750 The Chinese take over the state of Tibet. • 1789 The Social Revolution begins in France.	• 1815 Napoleon is defeated at the Battle of Waterloo. • 1839 The Opium War begins between Britain and China.	• 1845 The potato famine hits Ireland. • 1854 Russia is defeated in the Crimean War.

1900　　　　　　　　　　　　　　　　　　　　　　　1949

	1910	1920	1930	1940
EVERYDAY LIFE	• SAFETY RAZOR (1903) • WASHING MACHINE (1907)	• DOMESTIC ELECTRIC REFRIGERATOR (1913) • ZIP FASTENER (1914)	• HAIR DRYER (1920) • POP-UP TOASTER (1927)	• NYLON (1934) • INSTANT COFFEE (1938)	• AEROSOL CAN (1941) • MICROWAVE OVEN (1946)
TRADE AND INDUSTRY		• STAINLESS STEEL (1913) • ASSEMBLY LINE (1913)	• SYNTHETIC RUBBER (1927)	• POLYTHENE (1933) • PHOTOCOPIER (1938)	• NUCLEAR REACTOR (1942)
SCIENCE AND COMMUNICATION	• ELECTRO-CARDIOGRAPH (1903) • THERMIONIC VALVE (1906)	• NUCLEAR MODEL OF THE ATOM (1911)	• GEIGER COUNTER (1925) • ANTIBIOTICS (1928)	• ELECTRON MICROSCOPE (c.1931) • BALL-POINT PEN (1938)	• CIRCUIT BOARD (1943) • COMPUTER (1946) • TRANSISTOR (1947)
TRAVEL AND EXPLORATION	• DISC BRAKES (1902) • WRIGHT FLYER (1903) • CAR SEAT-BELT (1903)	• ELECTRIC TRAFFIC LIGHTS (1914) • WINDSCREEN WIPERS (1916)	• MOTORWAY (1921)	• JET ENGINE (1930) • CAT'S EYES (1935) • RADAR (1935)	• RADIAL-PLY TYRES (1949)
ENTERTAINMENT AND LEISURE	• MECCANO (1901) • TEDDY BEAR (1903)		• TELEVISOR (1926)	• ELECTRIC GUITAR (1932) • STEREO RECORDING (1933)	• SCUBA (1942) • LONG-PLAYING RECORD (1948)
WORLD EVENTS	• 1901 Marconi radios across the Atlantic. • 1904 Work starts on the Panama Canal.	• 1914 World War I breaks out. • 1915 Einstein develops theory of relativity.	• 1920 Gandhi starts movement against British rule in India. • 1929 U.S. Stock Exchange crashes.	• 1936 Civil war starts in Spain. • 1939 World War II begins.	• 1945 Atom bomb destroys Hiroshima. • 1948 Policy of apartheid begins in South Africa.

1950				1999
	1960	1970	1980	1990
EVERYDAY LIFE • STEAM IRON (c.1955) • VELCRO (1956) • LYCRA (1959)	• TEFLON COOKWARE (1960) • FLYMO (1963)	• FOOD PROCESSOR (1971) • DIGITAL WATCH (1971)		• SELF-HEATING TINNED FOOD (1991)
TRADE AND INDUSTRY • CREDIT CARD (1950) • NUCLEAR POWER STATION (1954)	• INDUSTRIAL ROBOT (1962)	• BAR CODES (1974)	• SMART CARD (1982)	• NUCLEAR FUSION (1990s)
SCIENCE AND COMMUNICATION • BIRTH CONTROL PILL (1954) • SILICON CHIP (1959)	• COMMUNI-CATION SATELLITE (1962) • WORD PROCESSOR (1964)	• X-RAY SCANNER (1972) • PERSONAL COMPUTER (1978)	• POST-IT NOTES (1981) • ARTIFICIAL HEART (1982)	• VIDEOPHONE (1991) • VOICE RECOGNITION (1990s)
TRAVEL AND EXPLORATION • SPACE SATELLITE (1957) • HOVERCRAFT (1958)	• JUMBO JET (1969)	• CATALYTIC CONVERTER (1979)	• SPACE SHUTTLE (1981)	
ENTERTAINMENT AND LEISURE • TRANSISTOR RADIO (1954) • VIDEO RECORDER (1956)	• SKATEBOARD (1963) • CASSETTE RECORDER (1963)	• HOME VIDEO GAMES (1972) • WALKMAN (1979)	• RUBIK'S CUBE (1980) • COMPACT DISC (1982)	• VIRTUAL REALITY (1990s)
WORLD EVENTS • 1953 Scientists reveal DNA's structure. • 1953 Hillary and Tenzing climb Everest.	• 1966 Cultural Revolution starts in China. • 1969 U.S. astronauts land on the Moon.	• 1973 Australia's Sydney Opera House is built. • 1978 The first test-tube baby is born.	• 1986 Nuclear reactor explodes at Chernobyl. • 1989 The Berlin Wall comes down.	• 1990 Iraq invades Kuwait. • 1991 Slovenia and Croatia announce their independence.

Resources

ENGLAND

B.T. Museum (Museum of Telecommunications)
145 Queen Victoria St.
London EC4V 4AT

Birmingham Museum of Science and Industry
Newhall Street
Birmingham B3 1RZ

Bradford Industrial Museum
Moorside Mills
Moorside Road
Bradford BD2 3HP

The British Museum
Great Russell Street
London WC1B 3DG

Duxford Air Museum
Duxford Airfield
Cambridge CB2 4QR

Eureka! The Museum for Children
Discovery Road
Halifax HX1 2NE

Exeter Maritime Museum
The Haven
Exeter EX2 8DT

The Exploratory (Hands-on Science Centre)
Bristol Old Station
Temple Meads
Bristol BS1 6QU

Fox Talbot Museum of Photography
Lacock, near
Chippenham
Wiltshire SN15 2LG

Great Western Railway Museum
Faringdon Road
Swindon
Wiltshire SN1 5BJ

Greater Manchester Museum of Science and Industry
Liverpool Road
Castlefield
Manchester M3 4FP

Horniman Museum
100 London Road
Forest Hill
London SE23 3PQ

John Jarrold Printing Museum
Jarrold Printing Company
Whitefriars
Norwich NR3 1SH

Leicestershire Museum of Technology
Abbey Pumping Station
Corporation Road, off
Abbey Lane
Leicester LE4 5PX

London Transport Museum
Covent Garden Piazza
London WC2E 7BB

Museum of the History of Science
Broad Street
Oxford OX1 3AZ

Museum of Mankind
6 Burlington Gardens
London W1X 2EX

Museum of the Moving Image
South Bank
London SE1 8XT

Museum of Transport
Boyle Street
Cheetham
Manchester M8 8UL

National Maritime Museum
Romney Road
Greenwich
London SE10 9NF

The National Motor
Museum
Beaulieu
Hampshire SO42 7ZN

National Museum of
Photography, Film,
and Television
Pictureville
Bradford BD1 1NQ

National Railway
Museum
Leeman Road
York YO2 4XJ

Newcastle Discovery
(Museum of Science
and Engineering)
Blandford Square
Newcastle NE1 4JA

Prescot Museum of
Clock and Watchmaking
34 Church Street
Prescot
Merseyside L34 3LA

The Robert Opie
Collection (19th-20th
century packaging)
Albert Warehouse
Gloucester Docks
Gloucester GL1 2EH

Rural History Centre
The University
Whiteknights
Reading RG6 2AG

The Science Museum
Exhibition Road
London SW7 2RL

The Wellcome Museum
of the History of
Medicine
Exhibition Road
London SW7 2RL

Whipple Museum of the
History of Science
University of Cambridge
Free School Lane
Cambridge CB2 3RH

WALES

Swansea Maritime and
Industrial Museum
Museum Square
Maritime Quarter
Swansea SA1 1SN

Welsh Industrial and
Maritime Museum
Bute Street
Cardiff CF1 6AN

SCOTLAND

Museum of Flight
East Fortune Airfield
Athelstaneford
East Lothian EH39 5LF

National Museum
of Scotland
Chambers Street
Edinburgh EH1 1JF

University of Edinburgh
Collection of Historic
Musical Instruments
Reid Concert Hall
Bristo Square
Teviot Place
Edinburgh EH8 9AG

IRELAND

National Transport
Museum
Howth Castle
Dublin 13

R.T.E. Broadcasting
Museum
29 Lower Rathmines Rd.
Portobello
Dublin 6

Ulster Folk and
Transport Museum
153 Bangor Road
Cultra
Holywood BT18 OEU

USEFUL
ADDRESSES

The Patent Office
25 Southampton Bldgs.,
Chancery Lane
London WC2A 1AW

W.H. Beck Greener and
Co. (Patent advice)
7 Stone Buildings
Lincoln's Inn
London WC2A 3SZ

Index

Index of inventors

Acknowledgements

Dorling Kindersley would like to thank:
Heather Blackham, Kate Eagar, Myfanwy Hancock, and Carlton Hibbert for design assistance. Elise Bradbury and Anderley Moore for editorial assistance. Caroline Potts and Robert Graham for picture research assistance. Hilary Bird for the index.

Photographs by:
Paul Bricknell, Martin Cameron, Peter Chadwick, Andy Crawford, Philip Dowell, Mike Dunning, Philip Garwood, Steve Gorton, Ralph Hall, Peter Hayman, Chas Howson, Colin Keates, Gary Kevin, Dave King, Kevin Mallett, Ray Moller, Stephen Oliver, Daniel Pangbourne, Barry Richards, Tim Ridley, Dave Rudkin, Karl Shone, James Stevenson, Clive Streeter, Matthew Ward, Adrian Whicher, Jerry Young, Michel Zabé

Illustrations by:
Russell Barnet, Rick Blakely, Peter Bull, Kuo Kang Chen, Stephen Conlin, Luciano Corbella, Nick Hewetson, Ray Hutchins (Linden Artists), John Hutchinson, Stan Johnson, Helen Lee, Jason Lewis, Louise Morley, Sergio, Taurus Graphics, Eric Thomas, Richard Ward, Gerry Wood, John Woodcock

Picture credits:
t = top b = bottom c = centre l = left r = right

The publisher would like to thank the following for their permission to reproduce their photographs:

Birmingham International Airport Photo Library 107b; Black & Decker 27t; Bridgeman Art Library/Royal Geographical Society 117r; British Library 89r; British Museum 48c; J. Allen Cash Photolibrary 47tr; Bruce Coleman: John Worrall 22–23, Gene Ahrens